SECRETS

OF A

Simple Man

JOHN DETERMAN

outskirts press

Introduction

I decided to write this book after reading a book written by a great Oklahoma football player in the 80's. I thought his book was okay, but I felt I had a lot more interesting stories than he did. I thought my family and friends might enjoy it. Also, as I met people throughout my life and shared some of my stories, I often heard, "Man, you should write a book!"

There are some stories that I have never shared with anyone. I didn't think it would be good if someone knew too much about me. It might give them the upper hand in one way or another. So, I kept a lot of secrets. This book is my attempt at finally being transparent.

Enjoy it with laughs, tears, and maybe some memories of your own. And, by the way, the statute of limitations has expired on all activities mentioned!

DISCLAIMER: This is **MY** recollection of events!

Table of Contents

Introduction

1. I Was Innocent 1
2. It Wasn't My Time 10
3. The Tough Guy Act 22
4. He Was My Best Friend 30
5. True Love 51
6. Joltin Johnny 58
7. A Dream Come True 70
8. To Protect and Serve 84
9. More Crazy Memories 102
10. Conclusion 117
11. Favorites 118

I Was Innocent

I HAD IT pretty good growing up. I was adopted from an orphanage when I was six months old. My family lived in Omaha for a few years before moving to Columbus, Nebraska, where I spent the rest of my growing up years. Our neighborhood, called West Parkway, was the best a kid could wish for. There were lots of curvy streets with a big perfect circle block right outside our house. There were lots of hiding places, and islands with bushes, throughout the hood. This neighborhood would prove to be the setting for many significant childhood events and pranks in the years to come.

My parents were great. They made sure I had no worries. Dad was an army veteran and a heavy equipment traveling salesman. He made a good living but spent a lot of time on the road and rolled in really late many nights. My mom was a great homemaker and the best mom in the world. Her cooking was to die for. There was a hot dinner on the table every night. She loved helping people. She was passionate against abortion. During the Roe v. Wade era, she paid to have a bunch of bracelets made, and handed them out to people at the city park. She was heavily involved with the local protests. Mom also loved animals. She drove my dad nuts taking in strays!

I had twin sisters, also adopted, that were six years older than me, and an adopted brother six years younger. Because of the age differences, none of us really hung out much, except when my sisters were baby-sitting. I made sure they earned their babysitting money! LOL

For me, mowing lawns and a paper route were the best ways to earn money, although I'm not sure what I thought I needed it for...my parents gave me all I needed. Snow days were special...no school, and an opportunity to make a bunch of cash! My friends and I could make $50 or $60 in a day. We scooped until lunch, and then showed up at my house hungry and cold. Mom always took care of us with a hot lunch and cocoa.

My grade school years were good. I experienced the common kid struggles, such as wondering if girls liked me even though I had pimples! Of course I had the added bonus of a freckled face too.

I remember grade school as more of a social event. We just survived the classes and waited for recess. I didn't get into a lot of serious trouble, like kids today that have no respect for authority. I was the poster child for what people call an "ornery kid".

I loved life. My early memories were with a neighbor named Mike R. We hung out at a grocery store right behind Mike's house. Setting up our GI Joe's on dirt hills and firing at them with dirt clods and firecrackers was a blast, literally. A can of pop and a five-cent bag of sunflower seeds satisfied us for hours as we sat on top of a Goodwill box and watched people come and go. When the store closed, the parking lot was ours.

Once, we had this brilliant idea to try knocking each other off our bikes with the huge Sunday paper. It must have weighed five pounds. One of us positioned ourselves on the side of the lot with the newspaper, while the other raced through on his bike as fast as he could. We waited for just the right moment to hurl the newspaper, trying to knock the other one off his bike. We were like knights on horses! I was so small that I crashed just about every time I got hit. It was crazy fun!

In the winter, Mike R. and I built forts in the mounds of snow made by the loaders clearing the parking lot. We took snacks so we could stay all day. We started at the very top and dug fox holes. We made escape tunnels, just in case we needed a quick getaway. As cars left the parking lot we chucked snowballs at them. I'm amazed we didn't cause any blue hairs to wreck. Drivers circled the lot looking for us, but we were too slick.

Another favorite hangout spot was full of mulberry trees. We ate berries in our tree forts for hours. That's where I first broke the law. Stanley and Dennis, a couple of older friends, had a pack of cigarettes. They were Kool Menthols. I'll never forget it. Just a couple of puffs and I was dizzy and sick for some time. It was horrible. I didn't do it again until I was much, much older.

A different Mike, Mike A., was my accomplice at other times, later in grade school, and he became a long-time buddy. He and his dad did a lot of duck hunting. His dad was a taxidermist and we loved to watch him work. We had adjoining paper routes for several years. We helped each other finish quickly so we could hang out afterwards.

For the most part I didn't do a lot of vandalism, but I did have a small spree. Mike A. and I had a clubhouse above my garage. Along with a few other friends, we decided to fix it up. Our marvelous choice of decoration was car emblems. We used our pocket knives to carefully pry the emblems off of the cars. We had Monte Carlos, Cadillacs, BMWs,... nothing but the best, lining the walls of the garage attic fort. I wonder what happened to them? Maybe they're still above the garage of that old house.

Of all the shenanigans we pulled, "canning" probably caused the most damage. Canning was done by tying a piece of fishing line to trash can lids on opposite sides of the street. These were the good ole metal trash cans. Drivers couldn't see the string, and drove right into it, causing the lids to simultaneously slam into both sides of the car as they were drug down the street. What a riot!

Mike A. and I were also bombing buddies. In fact, he was my partner in crime for one of the worst bombing experiences of my childhood. The ammo of choice on this day was snowballs. We were bombing from the alley of his block. There was a great blind spot for drivers. We perfected the timing of our throws from the sound of the cars coming down the street. If we lofted it just right, we hit the windshield. That was a prize shot!

On this particular day, after several positive hits, I heard a car coming and timed my shot. As soon as the snowball left my hand, the driver of the car looked directly down the alley. It seemed like the snowball was in slow motion as our eyes met. The driver and I stared at each, for what seemed like an eternity, before the loud crash of another perfect windshield shot. I froze! The driver was staring at me like a rooster pheasant down a row of corn. He recognized me, and I recognized him. IT WAS MY DAD! He slammed on his brakes and made his tires squeal. My natural instinct was to run. I got to some apartments by Mike's house and saw my Dad come around the corner. I jumped in the bushes. Wouldn't you know, he parked right in front of the bushes where I was hiding. He just sat there, and sat there, and sat there! I was sure he must have seen me and was waiting me out. After the longest 10 minutes of my life, I walked out slowly, with my head down like a defeated warrior. It was not a fun ride home, or a pleasant dinner that night. I don't remember the punishment, but I probably got grounded for a week or so. I'm sure we were back in the alley in no time, doing the same thing.

Then there was Brian. We started hanging out around fifth or sixth grade and are still friends 50 years later. In fact, I set him up with the girl who is now his wife! As kids, during the summers, we were either golfing or fishing. I started golfing on Saturday mornings with my dad, and then Brian bought a set of clubs from him. Looking back at that now, those clubs were probably really big for Brian. We played several times a week at Vanburg's Golf course in Columbus. Sometimes we got a ride there, but most times we put the clubs on our backs and rode our bikes. It was all the way on the other side of town.

Brian never really played any other sport. He was on the high school golf team with Mike A, and continued golfing his whole life. Now he is a a certified pro and manages the prettiest golf course in Nebraska. He is one amazing golfer, and friend, for that matter.

Brian and I always did really well fishing too. We went to Wagner's Lake across from the golf course to catch bass, or fished the golf course ponds for huge carp. Once in a while we went to Lake North. My mom would drop us off so we could fish all day. I caught a master angler crappie there. It weighed 2.2 pounds.

Brian and I were good together. We pulled off the best bombing attack ever. We were trying to catch a car that kept driving through and tearing up the yards in my West Parkway neighborhood. We hid in a great spot under an evergreen. We saw a green Chevelle slowly pull up on the curb. This was it! They were going to do it!

One minor difference in this bombing incident was the artillery. We were going for destruction on this day. We used baseballs, rather than snowballs or tomatoes.

The car started spinning its tires through the yard, throwing up grass and dirt, so we hurled our baseballs. One went over the top of the car, but the other was a direct hit in the middle of the windshield. I'll never forget the sound of the glass shattering. The car slammed on its brakes right in the middle of the yard and came to a standstill. Brian and I looked at each other, and started running as fast as we could. I couldn't get the sound of the shattering glass out of my head as we tore through backyards trying to find refuge. We got away safely. The mission was a success. There were no more yards driven through for a long time.

Another mission, not so successful, happened one warm winter day after a good snow. The sun was shining and melting the snow, but, in the meantime, it made great snowballs. At recess, I was in the church parking lot, looking across the street at the high school. I noticed some windows opened on the third floor. I saw a teacher look out every few minutes, so I knew there was a class in session. I made a snowball and flung it as hard as I could. Bull's eye! I made it in the window. As I stood, stunned that I had actually hit the target, the teacher came to the window and looked directly at me. I sprinted across the street to get lost in the crowd of students but didn't make it to the other side. As I was in the middle of the street, a car locked up its brakes and squealed. I was able to focus long enough to see it was a friend of my dad's. Soon I was lifted by a cold hard force... called a bumper.

I flew at least five feet before coming to rest in the middle of the road. The driver was very apologetic and wanted to call an ambulance. I managed to get to my feet and convince him I was fine, head spinning, eyes trying to focus. He agreed not to call an ambulance, but he insisted on calling my parents. Fortunately, my mom was the one who picked me up. Not a word was mentioned about the snowball, she just made sure I was OK from getting hit by the car. I was feeling pretty lucky, until I got home. That perfectly thrown snowball had gone directly into my sister's Biology class!

One of my last bombing adventures took place when me and some buddies were bombing cars by the public high school. We all nailed the same car at the same time. The car came to a screeching halt. Car doors flew open, and out the high-schoolers came.

I ran like never before. I jumped a fence and split off from everyone else. I was feeling pretty free, when I felt something grab my neck. It didn't feel like hands, but it seemed to snag my skin. The excruciating pain I felt brought me to a complete stop. I had been grabbed by an overgrown rose bush that was about five feet tall!

Something warm on my neck was moving down my throat and to my chest area. Blood covered my hand as soon as I touched it. I thought "Oh great, I'll be the first person to ever die from having his jugular vein cut by a plant".

At this point, I didn't care if I got caught or not. I went to the back porch of the house with the rosebush, and sat down, groaning. A sweet lady came to the door and gave me a rag.

A short time later, I met up with my posse. Nobody got caught, but I was done for the night. I had one of the nastiest shredded necks ever.

In grade school, it was always great when your name came up to deliver milk for afternoon break. Usually, a couple of boys delivered them. One day my buddy Ronnie and I went to the social hall and loaded up the shopping cart with about 50 cartons of milk. I was zig-zagging through the social hall with the cart, fast and crazy, showing off. I lost control and everything shifted. Suddenly the cart tipped and milk cartons went everywhere! Some of them busted open. We were in a panic! What if we got caught?

First, we needed to clean up all the spilled milk, and then we needed to replace the missing cartons. There was a janitor's closet in the same room, so we grabbed mops and did a hurry up job. We cleaned up the best we could, and then went back to the main fridge and took several replacements. Luckily, all deliveries were made on our watch, but someone later in the week had to be short several cartons. We didn't hear another word about it.

Ronnie and I were a couple of the toughest kids in school. Then there was Terry, who came from a family of 12 or 13. His whole family was tough! For the most part we all got along and ended up fighting older kids, but one time Terry and I had a showdown.

During a basketball game at recess, Terry said something to me, and my temper got the best of me. I kicked him in the butt. He turned around and came at me with that Irish rage in his eyes. I knew I was toast if I just stood there, so when he got in range, I threw a straight long right hand which landed solidly on his nose. It immediately started bleeding.

As the fight circle formed around us, one of the school nuns quickly stepped in and ushered us both to the office. We had to stay after school and say a bunch of "Hail Mary's" . After that, we had mutual respect for each other. I knew he was bigger and stronger, and he knew I could fight and was fast as a cat!

It wasn't uncommon for Ron, myself and Mike W (Herman) to be sent to the principal's office together. Once, Sister Edna, who happened to be Herman's aunt, had all three of us kneeling and saying Hail Marys together for something we had done. If we messed up we had to start over. Herman had terrible gas that day. Every time we were just about done, he farted. We would all bust out laughing and have to start over. It seemed like we prayed for hours.

I don't remember exactly how old I was, but one day I was alone in one of my ground tree forts. I was soon joined by a neighborhood girl who was kind of a bully. This fort was in one of the islands of bushes in the middle of our neighborhood. I don't remember any small talk, or any talk for that matter. But I do remember that she was bigger than me, and she held me down, and took off her clothes. She told me to take my pants off. I was frozen, so she did it for me. She climbed on top of me and made me have sex with her. Then she got up, put her clothes back on, and left. I sat there in a daze. I was kind of sick and believe it had long term effects on me. I wasn't sure if I was raped or not. Eventually, I went home and took a bath. Mom wanted to know why I was taking a bath in the middle of the day. I told her I thought I got into some poison ivy, and, in a way, I did.

CHAPTER 2

It Wasn't My Time

IN HIGH SCHOOL, I wasn't a great student. I did just enough to get by. I was totally satisfied with C's. I often took books home, but they stayed in my car overnight. One of my all-time favorite classes was Shop. Myself and several classmates had to drive across town to the public school for this class. Sty and Mark were the only ones old enough to drive. We played chase and had mobile snowball wars.

From my point of view, the purpose of high school, just like grade school, was to socialize. There were about 75 kids in my class. We did a lot of drinking together. A typical 'great night' was a tape dance, and a party at someone's house afterwards. Other times we just partied at someone's house while the parents themselves were out for the night. Mark's house was great because he lived on a lake. We could go for a boat ride or have a bonfire. I'm surprised we made it as long as we did without an MIP charge.

Many nights, Mike A. and I went to Fred's house to get primed before a dance. Fred or his girlfriend bought whatever alcohol we requested. We drank our alcohol, and then headed to the dance. We did this a lot before football and basketball games too. I'm not sure if the teachers didn't know our condition or just chose to ignore it.

Cruising was another favorite pastime in high school. I know I gave Mom and Dad many gray hairs during these years. My dad bought Mom a 1970 Cougar convertible and had it painted candy apple red. It was the sharpest car in town. Mom let me drive it to and from school sometimes, but this particular weekend, I did not have permission. I was 14 or 15, and Mom and Dad had gone somewhere for the weekend. The car was parked in the garage with the keys in it. My buddy and I were looking for some excitement. We decided he would time how fast I could make a lap around the block in the little red beauty!

It was winter, and a little slick, but the streets were pretty much clear. I backed the car out of the driveway and waited for the "go" signal. As soon as his flag hand went down, I took off! I made good time on my first lap, but I knew I could do better. As I reached the starting point in front of my house, thinking about how good my second try was going to be, I saw our neighbor standing on his porch. No! If he saw me driving, I was toast! I hit the brakes hard and fishtailed into the driveway. I got the car straightened out and headed for the garage. I was lined up perfectly when I hit a patch of ice. There was nothing I could do to avoid hitting the garage door.

I finally got the car inside the garage and assessed the damage, to both the car and the garage. It wasn't pretty! And, the neighbor saw it all!

When I turned 16, I bought my first car… a Ford Fairlane with a 351 Cleveland engine, for $800. It was quick! I could power brake it from one side of the school parking lot to the other. Tony and I did a lot of cruising in that thing. Tony moved to Columbus from Omaha my freshman year. We started out on the wrong foot, but later became friends.

One night Mike A. and I were cruising. We decided to hang out in the church parking lot across from school while a Friday night tape dance was going on. We saw Brian pull in and park. Feeling ornery, I drove up close to Brian and threw a handful of pennies at his car. Brian had a nice, sky blue Pontiac Bonneville. A bunch of the coins hit Brian's car as intended, and he got mad. He quickly put his car in gear to come after me. I tore out across the lot going north up 18th Avenue. Brian was right on my tail.

I sped up and then quickly turned down an alley. Looking in my rear-view mirror, I saw Brian and his Pontiac fishtail into the alley. I don't think he ever regained control. Seconds later, when I looked in my mirror again, I saw the entire bottom of his car straight up and down. I don't remember if he flipped frontwards or backwards, but it ended up on its top. He slid into a guide wire on a pole.

I stopped immediately, backed up, and parked. Mike and I jumped out and ran to Brian's car. The top was totally level with the rest of the car. I was sick. I just caused my best friend's death!

As engine steam hissed and dust settled, I got on my knees and tried to look in the car. At first, I couldn't see anything. Then, I saw what looked like two racoon eyes staring at me from underneath the steering wheel. Somehow Brian ended up between the seat and the floorboard under the steering wheel. He was alive!

Soon the police, fire, and ambulances arrived. The two police officers that showed up knew Brian and I from a couple of weeks prior. We had snitched on a couple of brothers breaking into my neighbor's car, and these officers were the investigators.

The car was totaled. No witnesses. No tickets issued. Brian ended up with only stitches in his wrist.

I was on the football team for a couple of years but didn't get much playing time. I never played basketball. The Scotus basketball team made it to the State Championships in Lincoln one year. My parents actually let me drive there to watch. Me, Mike and Bob. We partied all the way to Lincoln. When we got in town, I felt like doing something crazy. As we drove past an elementary school, I pulled up over the curb and started chasing kids on the playground with my car! I don't know how I didn't get caught, or why I would do such a stupid thing. Obviously, I was not in my right mind.

The state basketball tournament lasted a few days, so we, along with several others, got rooms at a Motel 6. We invited a bunch of people to one of the rooms and filled the bathtub with beer on ice.

As the night went on, we got louder. Above the noise we heard a sturdy knock on the door. It was the cops. We could see them through the peep hole. I was full of liquid courage, and stood inside the locked door, imitating Cheech and Chong. I kept singing, "Keep on knocking but you can't come in", followed by hysterical laughter. As we silenced everyone in the room so I could perform my imitation one more time, the door quickly and forcefully broke open. The motel manager used his master key. The police and manager rushed in and found all the beer in the bathtub. Fortunately, they just took our goods and kicked us out of the room. They didn't arrest any of us.

Boxing had always thrilled me. Dad introduced me to it, watching fights on the Wide World of Sports on Saturday afternoons. I decided to give it a try and trained for Pat S in junior high. We trained in the basement of an old, abandoned hospital that was cold as ice. We heated it with portable propane heaters.

I'll never forget my first fight! It was like something out of a movie. It was a tiny show, commonly called a "smoker", in Chapman, Nebraska, population 324. The ring was in the middle of a smoke-filled room and was surrounded by a bunch of hardworking farmer types who were ready to see some action. It was very crowded and smelled like sweat. At 95 lbs, I fought three hard rounds against a kid named Rusty, and won by decision. There was no better high, no better drug, than having your hand raised as the winner in the middle of the ring! I finished that junior high season with a 3-1 record, beating some guy twice, and then losing to a tough Mexican kid in front of my hometown crowd in a tournament.

After taking a couple of years off, I started training for Pat S again, as a junior in high school. This time we trained above the swimming pool at the YMCA. It was hot and humid, but great for losing and maintaining weight.

The Columbus Boxing team was a city team and had nothing to do with school. Pat was the toughest coach I ever had. He pressed us hard and made me mad many times. But when it came time to fight, we knew we were ready. I credit him and his toughness for much of my success.

This time around, I jumped into boxing headfirst and was very dedicated. Once I started winning, I became obsessed. We were required to run a couple of miles every day before school. I didn't show up to any parties until after I finished training, and even then, partook little, if at all. Mom said I was hard to live with. I was always cranky because I was dieting and trying to keep my weight down. It all paid off in the long run, as I won a lot of bouts, and started making a name for myself.

It was 1980, and I was competing in the 112 lb weight class. I got a chance to show off my skills in my hometown of Columbus. I was matched against a kid from the Downtown Boxing Club in Omaha. He was a tall bean pole that had muscles the size of my wrists. I remember thinking, "Oh, this is a perfect fight for my hometown crowd." I fixed my mind on the knockout punch.

When the bell rang, I stood flat-footed, waiting to land that big punch. Instead, he caught me flush on the jaw with a long right hand and dropped me to the canvas, right in the center of the ring. I couldn't believe it. I got up right away, before my head was really clear. I was able to survive the rest of the round. I went out the next two rounds and really boxed him and pulled out the win. That was a humbling lesson for me.

The time came for my first appearance at the District Golden Gloves. Back then, there were five or six districts. The district winners went on to the the Midwest tourney for a shot at Nationals. I was lean and mean and mad at the world because of dieting and the pressure I put on myself. I was in the most awesome shape of my life. I was ready. But when I found out I was matched against the champ from the year before, I was scared.

The fight was intense, and very close. During Round 2, I was cut above my eye. At this point, my confidence had grown. I knew I could hang with the champ, and I thought I might be able to beat him. The 3rd and last round was for the glory. I was bleeding, but I was going to win. The doctor got up on the apron at least twice to check my cut. I pleaded with him to let me continue. I ended up winning a split decision and was named the 112 lb District Golden Glove Champion! The crowd loved it. I couldn't believe it. I got a jacket and major recognition in the newspaper. My family was very excited too. This meant I would advance to the Midwest tournament in Omaha. This was the big time!

I had about three weeks to prepare for Midwest after the tough district fight. I needed to let the cut over my eye heal, while still trying to spar a little. I also needed to maintain 112 pounds, and I was getting real tired of it. The season and being dedicated was getting old. I wanted to chase girls and have some fun. But, I trained harder than I ever had before. I was trying to peak a second time.

Midwest was unreal. We went to weigh-ins at the Civic Auditorium in Omaha. I saw guys I had only read about in the paper. I was intimidated. Here I was, just 16 or 17 and a junior in high school. Some of these guys were 20 and 30 years old and had been to the Midwest tournament several times before. One of the top guys in my weight was Jerry Clooney. He was about 25 years old and had a club foot. I remember reading about his knockout power. Not who I wanted to be matched against first.

The day of the fight, I was nervous and couldn't rest. I wanted my mommy! When I walked out of the dressing room and saw 5000 fight fans, I had to pee really bad. I would be glad when this was over. I drew a Hispanic kid out of South Dakota named Martinez. In the second round, I got caught with a right hand that hit me flush on the jaw. I saw all 5000 people in one glance, as I buckled and went to the canvas. Getting back up, I tried to focus on the ref. He was counting, but I couldn't hear anything except the roar of the crowd. Just as the referee came into focus, he called the bout off. I was completely disoriented. I was mad that I went out like that, but, at the same time, I was relieved that it was over. I could still go back to Columbus with my head held high. Best of all, it was time to catch up on my lost social life, eat as much as I wanted, and have some fun. And that's exactly what I did!

The next year, as a senior in high school, I convinced one of my best buddies from the younger years, Mike A., to box for the Columbus team. Joe, from Petersburg, also joined the team. I didn't know it at first, but Joe was already a hell of a fighter. Mike and Tom, my coach's brothers and veteran team members, were my motivators. They were mature athletes. They were good at boxing, and also state champion wrestlers. So, we had a small team of dedicated boxers. We were all close enough in weight that we could spar each other. We worked out for two hard hours, five nights a week. We all lived and breathed boxing together.

One of my all-time toughest fights was in Albion, Nebraska, in front of a bunch of classmates and a girlfriend. I fought a guy named Jockey Jay. He really was a horse jockey that rode on the local circuit in Nebraska, but he could fight too. He didn't even train, and he could fight!

We boxed hard, bell to bell. It was an action-packed fight. He kept sucker-punching me on the breaks, time and time again, with no warnings from the referee. So, during a clench, I pulled him in and bit his shoulder. He stopped boxing, and started yelling at the ref, "He bit me, man, he bit me!" I just kept attacking him with a bunch of punches. The ref never intervened or warned me. It was a very close fight, and I knew it could go either way. Fortunately, I got the decision.

Our boxing team did well throughout the season and made it to the Midwest tournament. Mike A. drew Tommy, out of Hastings. Even though Mike had developed into one heck of a boxer, Tommy stopped him with a hard body shot. He was just at another level. Today, Tom and I are good friends and have officiated many amateur boxing shows together.

I drew Larvie out of South Dakota. He was a veteran and moved like a cat. Why did I always draw the top guns first? On the other hand, if I could beat this guy, it would be downhill.

I stuck with him well the first round and a half. I was competing at 119 lbs. now and I had a hard, fast right hand. But his experience, and punching from angles, took its toll on me. He was fast on his feet, and faster with his hands, and he was hurting me.

At the start of the third round, I knew I needed to finish strong if I wanted the win. We were both tired and grabbed onto each other. The referee said, "Break!" As I dropped my hands and backed up,

Larvie hit me with a crisp shot which not only stunned me, but even worse, cut me. The fans booed. I thought it was cheap shot too, but the referee didn't call him on it. I finished the round trying to keep blood out of my eye and protecting the cut from opening more.

I lost the decision. Larvie went on to the National tournament where I believe he went to the finals before getting beat. It was not until later that I learned he was rated 6th in the United States. It's probably good I didn't know that before getting in the ring with him. Mike S from our team also went to the National tournament that year and did very well.

Boxing taught me about dedication, discipline, pain, sacrifice and celebration. It's so much more than two guys in a ring beating each other up. Little did I know that I would spend 12 years as a boxer, and, later in life, more than 20 years as a coach and trainer.

Although I was focusing on boxing rather than school sports during my senior year, I joined the track team to keep in shape. The coaches convinced me to pole vault, and I was pretty good. But I wouldn't say I had a smooth season!

One beautiful Spring day, I was at track practice. I had survived a Biology test during school, and it felt good to be outside, warming up in the vault pit. The team had gotten a new pole, and I was feeling especially limber, and getting great lift.

On one of my runs, I got way up in the air, but didn't get the pole spring that I wanted. I came straight back down, landing in the pit headfirst. The pole vault coach, who was also my Biology teacher, came to my rescue. I laid there sprawled out, fading in and out of consciousness and choking on the sunflower seeds I had stuffed in my cheek. The cheat notes I had written on the palms of my hands for his Biology test earlier that day were totally exposed. Busted! They called my mom down to the track to take me to the hospital. She wasn't very sympathetic. I never went back to Track. If I wasn't kicked off, I was too humiliated to return.

Another day, as a high school senior, I got into some major trouble (I don't remember what for!). The school said someone would be contacting my parents. My temper got the best of me and I stormed out of school early. I knew I needed seclusion, so I hopped in my car and drove to my family's cabin on a small lake 15 miles out of town.

This cabin, which was really just a nice trailer with a screened porch, was famous for high school parties. The lake was great for fishing as well.

I hung out at the cabin most of the afternoon trying to figure out how to get out of the jam I was in at school. My conclusion was to do something to distract my parents' attention from what I had done. I decided I would have a car accident on my way back into town, to shift their attention from anger to sympathy.

On the way home, there was a stretch of several miles of gravel county road before reaching the paved highway. I didn't want to involve another car, so I decided the county road was best. My parents knew I drove a little crazy, so my story would be believable.

I took off down the road and actually put on my lap belt. I got going almost 70 mph, and then I intentionally started swerving. After fishtailing several times, I lost control and spun in a full circle before hitting the ditch. The car rolled over to its side and then, in slow motion, came back down on all four wheels.

Dust was everywhere. I could smell burning oil. The lap belt had kept me from getting ejected. I felt fine but had a small cut by my eye. As I sat there for a minute and gathered my thoughts I felt like I should be hurt worse in order to keep my parents focused on "poor me", and not what I did at school. I took the heavy end of the metal seatbelt and started hitting myself in the face near the cut by my eye.

A vehicle stopped to check on me about 10 minutes after I wrecked. By that time, I had a good flow of blood streaming down my face, so they called an ambulance. A short time later I was loaded and heading to the hospital.

Mom was already at the hospital when I was wheeled in. She asked me what happened. I acted all disoriented and talked real slow and said I must have hit loose gravel and crashed. The doctor told her I would only need some glue on the cut and that I had a concussion. A few x-rays and hours later, I was home.

My car got towed. We picked it up a couple of days later. It was dented up on the side it had rolled on, and needed an alignment, but, other than that, it drove fine. Mission accomplished.

On my last day of high school, I had party fever. I was leaving for boot camp in five days. Tony and I were in my car. We drank a couple beers. We ran into my dad not too far from school. We pulled into a parking lot and said hello. His last words were, "Be Careful".

Tony and my grandma lived across the street from each other a few blocks from school. In front of their houses Tony and I decided to play car chicken with a guy we knew. He drove into my lane, and I drove into his. It would have been a simple cross over, but as our cars approached each other, he turned CHICKEN and turned back into his own lane. I had two choices: drive into a lawn and hit a tree or take the crash head on. I chose the latter. We hit at about 25 miles per hour.

My car looked ugly and sounded worse. The radiator fan was hitting the shroud, making an awful noise. I could smell gas and antifreeze. I thought the car was going to blow up.

Tony bailed and ran to his house, literally yards away. I tried to run away from the car too, but my legs gave out and I fell to the ground. I had hit my head pretty hard on the steering wheel. Next thing I knew, the other driver was leaning over me, telling me how sorry he was. I grabbed him by the shirt and pulled him down to my face. I told him not to say anything about playing chicken or we could both get reckless driving tickets. I told him to say I just came over into his lane.

I heard a lot of sirens and saw a lot of people gather. My dad showed up. So did the police. Fortunately, a friend had removed any contraband from our car. I told the police I had dropped something and bent over to get it, and that's when I went into the other lane. No tickets were issued. They believed I was just another inexperienced teen driver.

It's amazing I survived those teen years. When I was 14, I decided I wanted to die. It was over stupid stuff like girls and pimples. I went to a favorite river spot with my Ithica 20-gauge single shot. I loaded my gun, said a prayer, and pressed the barrel against my chin. I cried and pulled the trigger. Nothing....no click, ...no bang....nothing. I had forgotten to pull the hammer back on the gun. They say what doesn't kill you makes you stronger.

CHAPTER 3

The Tough Guy Act

WHAT WAS I doing? Here it was, a week after my high school graduation, and I was flying to Fort Benning, Georgia for boot camp. I had joined the Nebraska National Guard.

I had become a little out of control my senior year. I needed discipline. It was for the best. I convinced myself it would make a great boxing training camp, minus the sparring and bag work. I'll never forget Dad's face as I looked out the window of my plane getting ready for take-off. He raised his fist in the air and tried to force a smile. I think he cried. I know I did.

When the plane landed in South Carolina, a bus was there to pick us up, me and about 75 other scared kids. My tough exterior was shaking in its boots. We were hauled to the reception station at Fort Jackson to stay for a few days before going on to Fort Benning.

Fort Jackson must be where the drill sergeants practice making you feel like a worm. They plant the fear in you right away! We had to learn their way of cleaning our rooms and making our beds. We had to get a haircut. I felt so fortunate to end up in the barber's chair next to a long-hair-hippie-looking dude that I had been watching since the airport. I couldn't wait to witness this guy, who I kinda thought was a dirt bag, get scalped! As it turned out, getting our heads shaved was quite a bonding experience. One look in the mirror and reality set in. His name was Osborne and he became my best friend and confidante at Fort Benning. We helped each other get through the hell. Today, when I get the ole' boot camp graduation book out, there are several other buddies that trigger great memories. Unfortunately, I didn't keep in touch with any of them.

My drill sergeants were tough, and I respected them. I took training seriously. We were at the "Home of the Infantry" and the ranger jump school. More than once it entered my mind to go full-time and become an Airborne Ranger. I often wonder what life might have been like if I had.

After eight weeks of basic training, I moved to a specialized training area. I was in Mechanized Mortars. There wasn't a big change in routine. The typical day required getting up at 0430 and running several miles, then calisthenics for about a half hour and a run back to camp for breakfast. We couldn't talk while we ate. I was always getting in trouble in the chow hall. We had to eat fast and get back to the barracks to prepare for the day, which might consist of any number of torturous things.

Many times, we spent several days bivouacking. Bivouacking is kind of like camping, but with no luxuries. We didn't get a shower unless we were staying in the field longer than five days. When we finally got a shower, a big truck full of freezing water was rolled in. I have to admit though, freezing or not, it felt great to get all the dust and red clay off!

There were times that seemed unbearable. After training hard all day, trying to sleep was a challenge of its own. We slept in tents with quite an assortment of insects that called the area home. Once, in the middle of the night, a fellow soldier started screaming at the top of his lungs.

Osborne and I found our flashlights and hurried out of the tent. Almost everyone else did the same. He had gotten up to take a leak, not realizing he had stopped on an ant hill to urinate... a fire ant hill, that is! His leg was totally devoured. He got medevacked back to camp.

A week later I did a similar thing with an ant hill, but I reacted quickly when I felt my foot on fire. For a couple of days, Osborne couldn't help but laugh every time he saw me limping around because of the swelling. He had no idea what kind of pain I was in! Looking on the bright side, I was so grateful I didn't get the scorpion in my sleeping bag. That earned one of our guys an airlift out of the field. He got stung several times.

Another incident that sticks out in my mind happened during a forced road march. A heavy-set kid kept falling behind. He couldn't stand the heat. Eventually he fell out. A drill sergeant ran over to him and started kicking him in the ribs, yelling at the top of his lungs to "get up". I looked back and wanted to go knock that sergeant out, but I kept going. We looked for the kid when we got to our destination, but he was never seen again.

It didn't take long for word to get around that I was a boxer. There were a couple of guys in my platoon that were also from Nebraska. They had heard of me and confirmed my boxing abilities to any of the non-believers. Occasionally, I liked to shadow box at night in the barracks, or throw punches while doing morning run, if the drill sergeants weren't looking. I got in great shape and even earned the Army Physical Readiness Award. I got a three-day weekend pass for my accomplishment.

Two of us earned the pass. The other guy wasn't from my unit, so I ventured into Columbus, Georgia.... alone. What an experience! It's kind of foggy, but I remember three main things: I drank a lot, I got a tattoo, and I got stabbed.

It had been a couple of months since I had any alcohol, so it didn't take long to get wasted. I really don't even remember where I stayed, or if I checked in anywhere. It was a total miracle that I made it back to Ft. Benning on time.

Tattoos were strictly forbidden during boot camp. The government owned us now. Besides, it would be really sore, and couldn't be in the sun. Nevertheless, in my altered state of mind, I decided to cover the homemade tat on my arm with my mom's favorite flower... a rose.

The second day on pass, I went to a bar that was filled with primarily locals, and a few military men. It had one of those mechanical bulls. It was a riot to watch the drunks get thrown off. After enjoying the fun atmosphere for about an hour, I went to the restroom. As I was relieving myself, the door opened, and the lights quickly went off. Within seconds, a punch hit the right side of my face. It wasn't a solid shot, but I could tell it was a big, heavy fist. Then there were more, many more. I figured there was no less than three guys hitting me simultaneously. After getting caught with a few blows, I unloaded about an eight-punch combination in all directions. I could feel that I had connected with some facial bones. Then, I felt a sudden warm sensation. I grabbed my hip and pulled away a hand that had stabbed me. I dropped to the floor and started feeling my way through and around legs. I was getting kicked but was crawling for the crack of light at the bottom of the door. When I got to the door, I jumped up and yanked it open. I ran out the back to the alley and sprinted as fast as I could around the corner. Between the adrenaline, being scared, and wondering how bad my hip was, I was barely able to breathe. I thought I might hyperventilate right there!

Looking down at my leg, blood was soaking through my jeans from hip to ankle. How bad was it? Will I pass out? Am I loosing too much blood? These guys must have thought I was easy prey... a GI all alone in a club. They were probably planning to rob me. But they didn't get a dime! I decided I should run some more. I didn't know who these guys were, and I wasn't planning on finding out. I just wanted to get away.

I ran into the bathroom of a little gas station to check myself out. The stab wound was on my right hip. It was about an inch long, and I don't think over an inch deep. Wow! I was so lucky! Before leaving the store, I bought gauze, bandaids and tape, and fixed myself up.

When I got back to the base and showed Osborne my tattoo and my stab wound, the first thing out of his mouth was, "How are you going to hide that?" Hmm, I hadn't thought about that! My arm was sore and swollen from the tattoo. It was on my shoulder where it was covered by my shirt during the day. The biggest problem was keeping it hid in the shower area so I didn't get snitched on. My hip was sore and swollen from the cut also. Somehow, I found a way to keep both a secret. No one knew except Osborne.

Many times, the mode of transportation to our daily training site was a semi-trailer. It was horrible. Not for the claustrophobic. We were packed like sardines, sometimes as long as 30 minutes. One morning, a brother from Chicago decided to swat the back of my head. He was about two feet above me because he was standing on the bench along the edge of the trailer. Between bumps and trying not to drop my rifle, I hit him as hard as I could in the solar plexus. He let go of his rifle and dove for my head. I struggled to stay on my feet. I knew if I went down in this trailer, I would get crushed. It was too crowded to get another punch off, so we just grabbed any body part we could get our hands on. Fortunately, I got his prize and was able to negotiate! I squeezed and pulled and squeezed and pulled until someone finally convinced me to let go. The rest of the trip he knelt down and stared straight ahead. Now, he was officially one of my haters.

After that, we co-existed without incident, until one night outside of the barracks when we were cleaning our weapons. He was running his mouth, and so was I. I didn't take any crap from him (the story of my life!), even though he was much bigger. I'm not sure what the last straw was, but he threw the first punch. We started boxing, without gloves of course! He had a jab like a hammer. He was so much taller than me. When I tried to get on the inside, I got hit three times to his one. I was kind of embarrassed because he was landing some great shots, and my reputation as a decent boxer was at stake. I finally got to the inside and landed a hard right hand/left hook combination that staggered him and made his lip bleed. No sooner did I back out, hands still up, when I heard the drill instructor yell, "Determan that's it!"

Both of us got threatened with Article 15's and barrack restrictions. We ended up with KP special duty. My special duty was cleaning all the ovens in the chow hall until they were spotless… with a toothbrush! I started after the evening chow. By the time I finished, everybody else was in the rack. I had about three hours to get some sleep.

Mail could be the worst part of the day, or the best, depending on if your name got called, and who the mail was from. Other than the weekly letter from Mom (which definitely kept me going!), there were two days that I very distinctly remember getting special mail. The first day I got a letter saying I was in trouble for not filing a state accident report for the car wreck I had the last day of school. The second was my 18th birthday. When I woke up that day, realizing that I was at boot camp was totally depressing. That is, until the mail came.

We were scheduled to start a 15-mile forced road march with simulated ambushes and combat that night. This was going to be one of our toughest exercises for the year, and it was happening on my birthday. Mail call was after chow, and a couple hours before heading out. We stood in formation as the drill instructor called out names. There it was…I had mail! It was a birthday card from mom and dad. What?!

My name got called again! This time it was from a high school friend, not necessarily someone I would expect to get a letter from. He sent a nice surprise!

The road march wasn't as bad as I thought it was going to be. We had a few laughs along the way. The night was totally dark and still. Osborne kept lifting the helmet off my head with his M-16, sending it banging down the road. "Who the hell is that?", my drill sergeant screamed. I didn't say a word. I didn't want a face-to-face confrontation with my DI! After about the third time, it was inevitable. He dressed me down, totally. I wanted to punch Osborne. But other than that it was a fun night. I was totally shot when the sun came up, but I made it.

Between calling my family and my girlfriend, I ran up quite a phone bill. My mom was in poor health. I didn't really know if I would ever see her again. She had already been diagnosed with stomach ulcers several years prior, and recently had a cancerous tumor removed. I begged God not to let her die before I saw her again.

I was also missing my girlfriend. Trying to make a girl, just out of high school, wait around for me for three months really sucked. Many times, she didn't answer when I called her. My buddy Brian was my informant. He kept me updated on what she was doing. One time he was hesitant, but finally broke down and told me he had seen her with another guy a few times. I already didn't care for this guy very much, and now I couldn't wait to get home and tear his head off. I sent that message to him via Brian before I got home.

Although I gave the impression I was tough, most of the time at boot camp I was full of fear and loneliness. I was afraid I would be recycled and have to complete basic training again. I was afraid I wouldn't see my mother again. I was afraid someone would find out how afraid I was. I was also very lonely.

Even though I had grown up in the Catholic school, I felt like I had actually just started a real relationship with God at boot camp. I went to church whenever I could and prayed often.

Graduation day finally came, along with quite a mixture of feelings. I was jealous...jealous of those who had girlfriends and family fly in for the event. I was excited...excited to get back home. I was relieved... relieved that the fear and loneliness was over. I was proud... proud of my accomplishment. I was overwhelmed with emotion. I cried.

CHAPTER 4

He Was My Best Friend

WHEN I GOT back to my hometown of Columbus, Nebraska, from bootcamp, I felt mentally and physically tough. I had matured. No one else in my high school class had gone directly into any Armed Forces, so I felt I had experienced something none of them had, a lot like boxing. I was confident...maybe TOO confident.

I had a little time before starting the Spring semester of college and had plenty of money. This basically led to a month-long drinking binge. I drank, and bought rounds for everyone, spending almost $1000 in one month. I started working for a construction company to save a little bit, but I was spending so much I actually just broke even.

I still wasn't old enough to drink legally, but I went to my dad's hang-out and got served at will. They knew I wasn't old enough, but I guess they figured if I could go to boot camp, I could drink.

The bar was my second home for a couple of months. I got hooked on the barmaid, and her on me. She was several years older, but we seemed to click well. Dad didn't like it at all. Apparently, she had a fling with one of his married friends once. But, I didn't really care. I thought she was hot! As It turned out, I should have listened. She cheated on me. My crazy side came out when I went to her house to pick up a few things I had left behind. I stole her best bottles of wine and closed her cockatiel's head in its cage. It wasn't right, but it made me feel better at the time.

I was done playing around. It was a rough month, but it was time to put my newfound toughness to good use. Boxing season finally rolled around, and this was going to be my big year. I wanted to get in shape before starting college and training in Lincoln.

My dad helped our Columbus boxing club get into a new gym in a refinished barn. One night, while training, my coach Pat and my dad were watching Mike S and I spar. I don't recall what round it was, but he hit me with one of his famous body shots. I was totally paralyzed. I went down and experienced pain I had never felt before. I remember looking up from the floor, and seeing my dad standing at ringside, asking me if I was OK. I could tell by the look on his face, he was scared. I was too. I had never experienced this type of pain before, ever. I didn't know what it was, but I knew it wasn't normal. I thought Mike had split my spleen open.

As it turned out, I had mono and didn't know it. Going untreated, it had developed into a liver infection. I had a liver infection, and I had been pumping alcohol into it, like a tributary to a river, for the last few months! I wouldn't be boxing this year! I hung around and helped out at the gym a little, and then headed to Lincoln to start college.

Going to college was something I always wanted to do. That's part of the reason I joined the National Guard. They paid 75% of my tuition. Going to Lincoln, Nebraska, home of the Cornhuskers, made it even better. I was so pumped at first, but, looking back, I probably shouldn't have taken any classes my first couple of years. It was a heck of a lot of fun, but a total waste of money. I had to take several classes over, although I always did good in my Criminal Justice classes.

Some of my friends from Columbus had older brothers in one of the frats at the University in Lincoln. I thought it was pretty cool when they decided to rush me. Frats were known for their awesome parties, and I wanted to be included! I couldn't wait for the St. Paddy's Day party our house would host. I had gone to one at this same frat the previous year, when I was in high school. It would be packed with guys, gals and booze.

The frat promised they would not interfere with my boxing. But, it didn't take long for me to realize that we had differences! The first time I skipped the Monday evening formal dinner in order to train, I was called in front of the leadership. I had just completed one of the country's toughest boot camps, and I had very little tolerance for these three spoiled guys, who, by the way, wouldn't have lasted a day at Fort Benning. They talked to me like Ward Cleaver lecturing the Beaver. I listened very intently until they were done. I then proceeded to tell them that I felt I had to take legal action against the "house" for breaching our agreement. It was great! They were speechless as I walked out of the room. But, things only went south from there.

One memorable evening was a party we had off campus at a place called the Cherry Hut. I was either an idiot, or had too much to drink, but I let an upperclassman tell me I had to ride back to the frat in the trunk of his car. Me and another freshman were closed in the trunk together. The driver and his buddies tore around Lincoln, trying to bang us up. I was just hoping we didn't get into an accident. Knowing my luck, I'd get knocked out and hauled all the way to the impound lot, and still be locked in the trunk!

When the car finally stopped, and they let me out, I was totally disoriented. I was someplace I had never been before. My partner got shut back in and dropped off somewhere else. It took me a long, long time to find my way back to Campus. Walking hammered through an unfamiliar city is not good.

I was angry when I returned to the house. I didn't care for the driver who was responsible for my ride (and lengthy walk!), and I was determined to make him pay. As it turned out, I didn't have to. Shortly after dropping me and the other kid off, he ran a red light, got broadsided, and went to jail for DWI. Thankfully, no one was hurt in the wreck, but sweet justice! And I didn't get hauled away to the impound lot in a trunk!.

Hell Week, the main hazing time for freshman, was next. I didn't like it. One upperclassman asked me for a jellybean, and because I didn't have one, he wanted me to drop and give him 20 push-ups. Was this little weasel serious? I just laughed at him. They did all kinds of stupid stuff to us. They made us study, and not leave the house. When we did leave the house, we had to check out. They made us stay up long hours and then, when we finally got to bed, they would come in screaming and get us up to do more stupid stuff.

The second night of this crap they took us to the basement, a few at a time. One of the house guys appeared to be hanging. It looked very real and fooled me for a while. I finally couldn't take it anymore. I walked up to this guy hanging and hit him with a body shot. His reaction made him lose his grip on the noose, and he nearly did hang! It could have been an ugly, freak accident, for which I probably would have been charged with manslaughter. Once again, I got into a lot of trouble. The word at the house was that they were going to try to break me. I thought, "Oh boy, this ought to be good! These red-necked little punks are going to break ME?" I could hardly wait!

Instead of causing any more conflict, I started checking out of the frat in the morning and catching a nap in Elephant Hall when I wasn't in class. At the end of the day, I would go crash at my girlfriend's before returning to the frat. After a while, they quit doing any hell-week stuff to me. I think they had already made the decision not to keep me in the house, which was OK, because I didn't want to return the next year anyway.

The only frat guy I made friends with was Sanchez. He was a cool dude, from Scottsbluff, Nebraska via Illinois, who knew how to live. Sanchez had already been in the frat for a year or more. I think he enjoyed the frat for the same reasons I did...the parties!

One time I brought bad heat on the house during one of those awesome frat parties. Some big muscle-head and I got into it. I don't remember what his beef was about, but I do remember he had the nerve to follow me into my room in the middle of this packed party! I was in a no-win situation.

Sanchez jumped on his back to slow him down as he got closer to me. I went for my mace. The muscle-head had no idea what I was pointing at him until he was soaked. I must have sprayed half of a can at him. He lunged at me, saying he was going to kill me. Unfortunately, I had soaked my good friend Sanchez also. I slipped around them, in their disoriented state, and ran down the hallway.

I didn't say a word to anyone, but it didn't take long for everyone to figure out what had happened. The third floor, where my room was, had to be completely evacuated. It was a bit chaotic as people tried to escape the fumes. I bailed out the back door and hid for a minute to catch my breath.

Several of the muscle-head's friends came out. As they looked around, I bolted down the alley and across the street. I was drunk and scared! I went to my car and got a weapon. I hid out, like a panther in the woods, watching them. They never did find me.

I ended up breaking into a friend's house to stay for the night. When I got back to the frat the next day, nobody was happy to see me.

Those that would talk to me told me I was in deep stuff. They said this guy knew who I was, and he would find me. Oh great, I love sleeping with my eyes open! Once again, I had to meet with the frat board and the house mom over it. I claimed self-defense. That was my story and I was sticking to it.

I took Sanchez home to Columbus a few times. Although my parents were a bit leery of him, they really liked him. One particular week-end, there was a party at the frat, and Sanchez wanted to stay in Lincoln for it. I stayed around and partied with him for a while, but then decided to head to my parents' house in Columbus. Sanchez was insistent that I not go, but I wouldn't listen. I set off for home around 8:00pm. It usually took a little more than an hour to get there.

As I started driving out of Lincoln, I began hallucinating. Things got really weird, really fast. It didn't take long to realize that the reason Sanchez didn't want me to go was because he had slipped some-thing in my drink. Cars were coming at me a million miles an hour and looked more like little spaceships than anything else.

When I was a bit closer to my destination, I decided to take country roads so there would be less traffic. It just got worse. I got so lost that I didn't get home until 2:30 in the morning. I was never so glad to get somewhere in all my life.

I wasn't in bed long when I heard the phone ring. A minute later my mom came down to my basement room and asked me if I was OK? I told her yes, and asked her why? She said Sanchez was calling "concerned that I got home OK because I had been drinking before I left". What a dog! He dropped something in one of the few beers I drank, and then had the nerve to give my mom that line of crap! My mom thought he was a great guy to make sure I got home safe. At least he didn't tell her I left Lincoln at 8:00!

Once Sanchez and I had a few hundred sham raffle tickets printed up, and sold them at the female dorms and sororities. We said the raffle was for a ski trip in Colorado or something. Initially we did it for the money, but we ended up meeting a lot of girls, and of course they had to put a number and address on the tickets! I don't think any of them were the least bit skeptical about it either. Not that they had to be. We weren't creeps stalking them. Today you would never get away with it. I'm not sure about Sanchez, but I don't remember ever calling any of them. I had a girlfriend, and I must have been content.

Sanchez had it a little rough in the frat because he was an upperclassman that was supposed to be treating us freshman (especially me!) like crap. But we continued to be good friends. We weren't supposed to have any pets in the frat, but we both got those little, tiny turtles. Sanchez was a kleptomaniac and stole the turtles (among other things!) for us.

One afternoon, he and I were partying at the frat. Somehow, he locked me out of my room. We were laughing and having a blast! I decided I would show him, and went out in the alleyway and climbed up three stories of window air-conditioners. Before long I was looking in my window at his back. He was still standing next to the door laughing. I was able to open the fold-out window. As I prepared for my entry, I couldn't take it anymore, and busted out laughing. Sanchez swung around, looked at me, ran to the aquarium and scooped up a pitcher of dirty, nasty, turtle water. He began laughing again as he took a few steps from the tank to the window and let me have it!

I dropped three short stories and landed flat on my back on an air-conditioner, which was located directly next to the house mom's window. When I came to, I was being loaded on a stretcher. There were a lot of blurry faces. There were also a lot of paramedics, firemen, and cops. Of course, there stood Sanchez too, tight-lipped, with a fake look of concern on his face. I only had to spend 24 hours in the hospital. It was a good break from class.

The last day of the semester was a glorious day. It was beautiful weather and I had just finished my last final. Hundreds of students were walking around, partying, and loading cars to move home. Sanchez and I were in front of our frat playing frisbee. I had just opened my first beer.

Our frat house was on 17th Street, which always had a lot of traffic. After playing for a bit, Sanchez hurled the frisbee toward the street, and I ran after it. When I realized I wasn't going to be able to catch it, I tried to stop. My peripheral vision told me there were several cars coming. As I put on the brakes, my knee-high moccasins hit loose gravel. They seemed to give me extra speed, as I slid into the street, standing. I heard several people yell "Watch out!". It was a little late for that! I locked in on the driver's face that was about to squash me like a bug. It was a small car, but it hit me square. As soon as I felt the impact, I went airborne. I saw the parked Volkswagen, as I hit it like a rag doll. I'm not sure if getting hit by the moving car, flying into the parked car, or landing on the concrete hurt worse.

Within seconds there were a bunch of spectators. The driver of the car was in shock and didn't get out of his car for a while. My left side and leg hurt the most. As I laid there, I wondered if death was close. I felt like I must have had some internal injuries.

It wasn't long before I heard sirens. Sanchez came over and leaned down to talk to me. I remember him saying," JD, are you OK"? I just looked at him and groaned. But he couldn't keep a straight face. He busted out laughing, which made me laugh, and that hurt even more!

Soon a cop was standing over us, asking what happened. Sanchez, being the expert witness he was, said, "I don't' know, Officer, he just ran out into traffic". What a jerk! The cop then asked Sanchez if I had been drinking? Sanchez said, "Probably, it's after 10:00 a.m."

A short time later the fire department and ambulance showed up. They started to cut my pants off. I had just bought this new pair of jeans. I screamed at them not to cut off my new jeans! One of them said, "Look guy, there are hundreds of people standing around here. I don't think you want us to just take your pants off." I told him if they cut my new jeans, they would be buying me a new pair. He looked up at his partner and said, "Fine!", and took my pants off. I didn't realize how big the crowd was until I was on the stretcher. Traffic was backed up as far as I could see. I should have kept my mouth shut!

So there I was, the last day of school, back in the hospital. Go figure. As it turned out, my injuries were not all that serious. I was on crutches for a deep internal bruise to my thigh, and had a wrap around my bruised ribs. The doctor wanted me to stay 24 hours for observation since I had cracked my head pretty hard against the Volkswagen. I stayed around for about six hours, when Sanchez finally showed up. I got dressed, tore off my bracelet, grabbed my crutches, and went down a few floors to freedom. I remember hospital staff yelling that I was AMA as I walked out. I didn't know what that was. All I knew was that the frat was supposed to have one last party that night, and I wasn't about to miss it. We were outta there!

We spent a little time at our frat party and decided to road trip to Columbus for a wedding. As soon as we got to the wedding, Sanchez took one of my crutches and hid it. I got stuck all night sitting at a table with people I barely knew.

The next semester at school I lived in a basement apartment with two girls...my sister Deno, and the other whose name I don't recall. My mom helped us fix it up. The apartment got damp when it rained. If you stood in the kitchen, and touched something electrical, you often got shocked.

In the apartment across the alley was a girl I knew from Columbus. She was a couple of years older, but we were friends. She was chosen to do the All Big 8 Playboy shoot, so she was somewhat of a celebrity on campus. Hanging out with her was a little awkward. She dated a football player from Jersey City, named Stan. Stan and I also became great friends. He was a typical Nebraska football player. He was always broke and pawning things off, ...even his Nebraska football ring!

Stan took me to a couple of parties with some of the Husker players that were famous at the time. He also came to a couple of my boxing matches in Lincoln. I took him back to Columbus to meet all my dad's friends and hang out at the bar. He was a huge, cut, cool guy that could always make me laugh. I wish I wouldn't have lost touch with him.

Our basement apartment worked out for a semester or so, but I finally had to kick the other girl out. She was such a slob. I couldn't take it anymore! She constantly complained about how she couldn't lose weight, yet, every time I came home she had something stuffed in her mouth. She never did her dishes, and she said very little to me. I think Sanchez made her a bit nervous too. He came over often and give her a hard time. When I was training and watching my weight, I had little tolerance for people like her.

I heard that a friend of a friend was looking for a place to live. I trusted her, so I met them both for drinks one night and got introduced. I thought he was OK, so I let him move in. His name was Doug, and he was definitely different, but I couldn't quite put my finger on it. He was clean, respectful, funny, liked to party, and paid his rent on time. But something was odd. After a few weeks, I learned that he wore make-up. When I interrogated him about it, he said he was a model. He spent longer in the bathroom than my sister and I both!

Sanchez was leery of Doug too. The first time he met him, Sanchez thought he was a homosexual. Doug was the first person I met that could actually make Sanchez feel uncomfortable at times!

One night Sanchez and I decided to follow Doug when he left the apartment. I couldn't believe my eyes! He went into a gay bar. Chez kept saying "I told you so! I knew it!"

I don't know if Doug knew we followed him, but that night, for the very first time, he brought a "buddy" home with him. Sanchez and I were sitting in the living room, waiting to confront him, when the door opened, and he and his buddy walked in. This guy had tattoos everywhere, his eyebrows pierced, and different colored hair. He didn't stay long.

I really didn't know what to say to Doug, but Sanchez handled that. He said, "Johnny isn't living with no gay dude. You need to pack your bags and get out!" He looked at me, and I just nodded.

He was mad. He grabbed a knife and started wigging out and threatening us. He ran around the apartment until we chased him out.

He moved the next day. I really didn't have any hard feelings and I even helped him move. I took a lot of razzing from Sanchez though. He kept telling me that I had probably passed out a half dozen times, and Doug had his way with me. I refused to admit that was even a possibility.

One day after class, at that same basement apartment, Sanchez and I were sitting around getting primed. We let my pet rabbit out to run around, as we often did. We got distracted, and the next thing I knew, the rabbit was in the middle of the living room floor doing the "chicken". We were stunned as we watched it flip and flop on the floor like it was having convulsions.

We figured out the rabbit had eaten almost half of a poinsettia plant right in front of us. We discussed it for a bit. We came to the conclusion that it was a poisonous plant, the rabbit was suffering too much, and I didn't have any money for a vet bill. It had to die.

We stepped outside in our concrete stairwell area. I grabbed the nearest deadly weapon I could find, a good ole brick. I felt weird as I crushed that rabbit with devastating blows. I don't know what we were thinking. Of course, it made a bloody mess all around the entryway of the apartment. We cleaned it up as well as we could and threw the rabbit in the trash.

Not long afterwards, my sister Deno came home. Sanchez and I were still sitting in the living room talking about it. Gradually, she figured out bits and pieces. The rabbit was not in its cage. There was a crime scene, of sorts. She gave us a look like we had really lost our minds!

It seems Sanchez and I always had some type of pet around. He eventually got a pup. We took it to Columbus one weekend and left it with my mom while we went out on the town. It chewed two complete corners off our piano bench! Another time, he had this mutt at my apartment, and we were getting ready for the night. He had brought over some treats which we were going to partake in later that night, but the dog ate them. The dog went into convulsions too, but we didn't crush it with brick. Come to think of it, I'm not sure where that dog ever came from, or went to. It just kind of vanished.

One beautiful fall afternoon, Sanchez came to pick me up. We got primed and then decided to go to a friend's house. As he backed his Jeep out of the parking lot, he hit the neighbor's white picket fence.

He barely hit it, but a whole section collapsed. We proceeded down the street, and red lights came from everywhere. We continued driving long enough for me to chug the two beers we had opened. Sirens were blaring when Sanchez finally pulled over. The cops thought they were in a low-speed pursuit.

A female cop approached Sanchez, and she was not happy. As Chez looked for his billfold, he started smoozing and telling her she had to be the prettiest cop in the nation. She wasn't impressed. She got him out of the Jeep. I thought we were finished. She patted him down but didn't find anything. I couldn't believe it. She then had him do field sobriety tests. He passed. The only ticket he got was for leaving the scene of a property damage accident. Court was in two weeks.

The night before court we partied really hard, so I stayed at Sanchez's apartment. Besides, we needed to make up a good defense story for the Courts.

We forgot to set an alarm, and the next thing I knew, I felt sunshine on my face and looked at the clock. It was 0900 and we had court at 0930. I yelled at Chez to get up and get ready! We didn't even have time to shower. Immediately we were out the door and on our way. We found our courtroom just in time. When we walked in, court was already in session on another guy. I checked out the judge and, much to my amazement, it was a female. I remember thinking to myself, "We should be OK with the charm that Chez has with women".

A short time later, Sanchez was called to the front. The judge and the prosecutor read the facts of the police report. I was watching the judge as she eyed Chez up and down. It was now his turn to tell the story. He was on a roll, and his story was sounding good, when I noticed the judge get the strangest look in her eye. It was half sneer, half anger, as if she was trying to keep herself composed. Her eyes stared bullet holes at Chez as he carried on. She was very disturbed about something. There he stood, almost looking like a marine at attention, speaking ever so softly and innocently, as only he could. I thought he was probably far enough from her that there couldn't be a noticeable odor of alcohol. It was obvious he hadn't cleaned up for the event, but she had to know what busy schedules we had as college students.

As I studied her a bit more, she was locked in on his shirt. Then it hit me. It wasn't the fact that he had cotton mouth and foam in the corners of his mouth, and it wasn't that he was wearing the wrinkled shirt from the night before that he slept in. It was a Busch beer shirt. Not that having a beer shirt on was all that bad, but its what the shirt said... a light blue shirt with bold, black print, which read, "**To hell with your mountains, give me your bush".**

My body started to tremor and my legs got weak. Dehydration started to kick in. I got lightheaded and thought I was going to faint. Suddenly the judge interrupted Chez and said, "I think I have heard and seen quite enough. This court finds you guilty!" He ended up paying a fine for leaving the scene of an accident, and fixing the fence.

The next year, Sanchez and I finally moved into an apartment together. It was the top level of a house. It was about a 10-minute jaunt from campus. Sometimes we rode our bikes to school and other times drove a vehicle. Our landlord was a state trooper. He did not allow pets, but we ended up with a cat or two. Every time he stopped by, we had to scramble to hide them, but we never got caught.

It was Spring break and Sanchez and I were ready for an adventure. We wanted to rough it for a few days and live off the land, sort of a survival trip. We decided we wouldn't take any food, only a few snacks and a couple of bottles of liquor.

Sanchez knew of a spot near Scottsbluff Nebraska. He used to live out there and told me of an old rustic cabin in the middle of nowhere we could stay at. He told me of a creek that ran through the area and beautiful woods all around. This sounded like the ideal spot. Soon we would be sipping our drinks by the fireside, relaxing in what Sanchez called "God's country".

When we left Lincoln, it was overcast with temperatures in the 50's, a pretty average day for Nebraska in the Spring. We drove Sanchez's Jeep Cherokee and partied along the way. Scottsbluff was about a six-hour drive, not far from the Colorado border.

The farther west we went, the colder it got. Then came snow, a lot of snow. We were driving into a heavy storm. Looking back, I'm not sure why we didn't check the weather prior to heading out. We didn't have smartphones back then (1983 or 84?), so we listened to the radio for weather updates. They were not good! We were traveling on Interstate 80 and, at times the snow was so heavy we couldn't see the road.

When we got to Scottsbluff, it was clear we were in the eye of the storm. A good ole Nebraska blizzard. We had to leave the interstate and get on county roads to get to the cabin. The roads weren't plowed, so we put his Jeep in 4-wheel drive.

It was late afternoon when we reached a desolate road, and Sanchez pulled over. I asked if this was it and he replied, "I'm pretty sure". I tried to tell him that maybe we should just go into a town and get a hotel for the night and return in the morning to find the cabin. He blatantly refused and insisted that we hurry up because it was going to get dark soon.

The gray clouds continued to pound down the blinding snow. We loaded up our back packs, put on heavy clothes, grabbed our guns and started hiking to find the cabin. Every time I asked how far we had to go, he would say "a while". When I asked how long "a while" was, he wouldn't answer.

I was starving already and hoped to see a rabbit or pheasant or something during our hike. We walked and walked and seemed to get nowhere. I was convinced we were going in circles. I started to get cold, really cold. I couldn't feel my feet and my legs were cramping up. Sanchez stopped every several hundred yards, looked around, then said, "this way". I didn't trust his instincts.

I was ready to give up. I started looking for big evergreens to climb under and start a fire just to stay alive. I believe this was the coldest and weakest I have ever felt in my life. We had hiked several miles. I could hardly lift my legs anymore. Finally, Sanchez yelled, "There it is!". I looked where he pointed but didn't see any cabin. He assured me it's just "up here a ways". We hiked another several hundred yards and there it was!

We dropped our gear and guns in front of the cabin. Our guns were so frozen we couldn't have shot anything on the way, even if we had seen it. The cabin had a chimney. I prayed there was wood inside because we needed heat.

The cabin was dark and cold, but at least we were out of the wind and snow. We managed to get a fire started so we could thaw out and get unpacked. We were so hungry and weak that we had to get into our snacks right away. They were all gone in the first hour.

The cabin had a couple beds, a small kitchen area and fortunately, a couple pans. There was no electricity because we were so far off the grid. Luckily there were some candles.

After warming up, we finally sat down to relax. Just chatting, I asked whose cabin it was. Sanchez said he had "no idea". He and his brothers had found it years ago. Whenever they used it, they just left it as they found it. Great! This trip just kept getting better and better. So far, we almost froze to death, we didn't have any food, and now we were trespassing in a stranger's cabin that was almost out of firewood.

Well, what d'ya do? We partied and played backgammon while we made plans to stalk some game the next day. I loved to hunt. I started with my dad when I was young. Dad and I only hunted pheasants. We shot a lot of them. As I got older, I started hunting deer as well. This would be a hunt of all hunts. This would be a blast! Literally!

Morning came early. As I got out of bed, I could see my breath. The fire had burned out and was just smoldering coals. Though cold, I hoped it would be a better day. We were both starving and needed to find some wild game, sooner rather than later. Sanchez got me pumped up, telling me about all the wild game we were about to see and hunt. We got dressed and headed out the door.

The snow had stopped, and the sun was out. It actually felt warmer outside than in the cabin. I had visions in my head of a lunch with an array of wild game like rabbit, squirrel, pheasant and maybe even deer. We walked together, our guns ready, looking for tracks and listening.

After walking more than three football fields and not seeing a single track, my hope started dwindling. We went down by the creek convinced we would find tracks in the fresh snow at the bank...nothing. I couldn't help but think Sanchez had blown this whole "abundance of wild game" way out of proportion.

As we walked, I realized yet another mistake we had made. We both had .22 rifles. One of us should've had a shotgun. Rifles were fine for rabbits and squirrel, but that's about it. The chances of hitting anything that flies with a .22 rifle would be slim to none. If we saw a deer and shot it with a .22, we would be tracking it for miles and it may never die. How stupid of us.

When all hope was nearly gone, we suddenly saw some ducks circling the creek, looking for open water. We got behind some cover as they began to cup their wings to come in for a landing. It was only a small group, and they spread out when they spotted us, and started flying away.

We both shot numerous times. I stayed on one duck and continued to shoot as he flew away. Finally, down he went! As expected, Sanchez yelled out that he got one. He was famous for that, anytime more than one person shot at any type of game. I know for a fact, to this day, I killed that duck. After all, I received a marksman award with a rifle in boot camp!

We both raced over to the dead duck. It wasn't much, but it was food. We postponed anymore hunting to go start cooking our big game meal.

We got back to the cabin and cleaned the duck. Once the feathers were off it had to be the smallest duck I've ever cleaned. As we prepared to cook, we realized the oven didn't work and there wasn't a bit of seasoning in any cabinet. Nothing. Not even salt and pepper, let alone any flour. We had to settle for boiled duck on the stove. I'm not sure if it tasted more like leather or tree bark. It was oily and nasty, but it was food.

We hunted more that afternoon but didn't see a thing. This wilderness area that Sanchez said had more animals than a zoo was a farce. We decided to pack up and hike back to the Jeep. We talked about food all the way, deciding what we were going to eat. We settled on tacos... lots and lots of tacos.

Back at school, after Spring break, we continued to party, but this was actually one of our more serious semesters. One night Sanchez was studying hard, and I wasn't. I started messing with him. We got into a wrestling match. He finally lost his temper and pinned me against one of our big steam heaters. He was a lot stronger than me. I couldn't move. I ended up with burn marks on my back.

After college, Sanchez sometimes flew into Nebraska from North Carolina (where he was living), to deer hunt. Paula and I lived on an acreage in the country at the time.

One day Sanchez and I had taken a break from deer hunting and were road hunting for pheasant. Road hunting is illegal if you do it wrong. If you're driving and see a pheasant in the ditch, you have to be off the road when you shoot. You can't shoot over the road, or step on private property to shoot.

On this day, we were only two miles from my house, driving my 1988 Toyota pickup 4x4. We had our shotguns between us on the seat when, much to our surprise, a few turkeys crossed the road in front of us. They were out of season to hunt, but we didn't even consider that. We jumped out of the truck. Before I even got my gun loaded, Sanchez blasted one. He quickly ran down in the ditch to grab it. Now we had to figure out where to hide it. The only logical place we could put it was behind the bench seat in my small Toyota truck. We stuffed it behind the seat, and even had to move the seat forward slightly to make it fit. There was still a little bulge, but we didn't have far to go. We got situated and took off.

We were discussing how awesome it was and how lucky we were to get the turkey. As we came over a hill, there was a dark green pickup sitting there. We immediately knew who it was. We had seen it before. It was a game warden! As we crept closer, the green pickup's driver's door opened. My heart was in my throat. A lot of things raced through my mind: my job (I was a sworn State Corrections officer), losing my gun, expensive fines, hunting privileges lost, shame.

He stood next to his truck with his hand up signaling us to stop. We did. It was obvious we were hunters by the way we were dressed. He stepped up to my window, introduced himself, and told me to put my truck in park and shut it off. We were toast. He made some small talk, then asked to check our guns. Most game wardens start with that. If the guns are loaded, or not in a case, they have probable cause to look anywhere. They are considered state police.

Sanchez and I stepped out of my truck. The game warden sat in the driver's seat and inspected our guns. He had problems sitting comfortably, since my seat was so far forward to make room for the turkey. I could see the hump in the middle of the bench seat. Even though it was winter, and cold out, I could feel sweat covering my entire body.

After checking out our weapons, the game warden stepped out of my truck. He made some more small talk, checked our licenses, and sent us on our way.

As we drove away, we couldn't even talk. I drove directly to our house and pulled into the driveway and up to the barn. We were still in shock, but got the turkey out, cleaned it in record time, and got it in the freezer. I don't think we hunted anymore that day.

It's a miracle that I lived through these experiences with Sanchez, and I'm able to write these memories down. So many things could have gone just a little different. So many times that Sanchez might have instigated a reaction in me that could have been my last. So many times that ended in laughter, but could have ended in tears.

Sanchez befriended me at the frat. He slipped drugs in my drink. He threw turtle water in my face, causing me to fall three stories. He threw a frisbee in the street, causing me to get hit by a car, laughed at me, and told the cops I had been drinking. He threw my roommate out of my apartment, an apartment in which he did not live. He took me to a cabin in the middle of nowhere and made me hike miles in a Nebraska blizzard. He pinned me against a steam heater causing burns to my back. He almost cost me my career by shooting a turkey illegally. But, he was my best friend. We still keep in touch often and visit each other occasionally.

CHAPTER **5**

True Love

IN HIGH SCHOOL, I was voted "Least Likely to Get Married". I didn't like that! Although I didn't expect it to happen until maybe my late thirties, I always thought how great it would be to have a wife and children. I had a lot of girlfriends over the years, but no one that I would say I ever really loved.

It was Spring semester 1984 at the University of Nebraska in Lincoln, and I found the girl of my dreams. She was in my English class. She was small, with cherry blonde hair. I thought she was beautiful, but way out of my league. I tried to flirt with her a couple of times, but she wouldn't have it. I had another female classmate that I always sat next to, but I couldn't keep my eyes off Paula.

At the time, I worked as a bartender. One cold, snowy, winter night, a couple of hours had passed without a single customer. Finally, the door opened and in walked my dream girl from English class, with her friend. I couldn't help but notice how good she looked in her blue jeans!

Paula and her friend decided to play pool. After a while, I joined them. I couldn't get her to talk much so I kept free alcohol coming. I thought if I got them both drunk, I could score some points by driving them home.

While we played pool, we had some small talk and a few laughs. I could tell the alcohol was starting to loosen Paula up. Several games and pitchers later, it was closing time. I told them I would take them home because they were in no shape to drive, and I was sober. But, they threw me a curve! They had brought a cab to the bar! They had planned to go out, get drunk, and not drive!

I eventually talked them into saving their money and letting me drive them home. I don't think my convertible with no defrost impressed her much, but she still invited me up to her friends apartment to chow on leftover Taco Bell. We all loosened up a bit and I knew there was a lot of things I liked about her. As I was about to leave, I gave her a hug and little kiss or something, and she pinched my butt!! I was excited and knew I would call her. Game on!

A few days later I tried to call her. I didn't get an answer. I was sure she gave me a bogus number. I was bummed out, but I kept trying. Eventually I was able to reach her. It turned out she had gone out-of-town for a few days for job interviews. She would graduate in a couple months.

We lined up our first date to go to my friend's birthday party. I went to pick her up at her basement apartment on Peach Street. As it turned out, we never made it to the party that night. In fact, we never left her apartment. However, contrary to my nature at that time, we didn't have sex! We really hit it off though.

We spent a lot of time together and slept together for a long time with me pressuring her for sex, but she wouldn't allow it. It was very out of character for me to continue to spend a lot of time with a girl that wouldn't give it up, but she was different, and I cared for her in a different way than I had anyone else. I knew she was worth the wait.

A short time later, we took her little Chevette on a road trip to Atchison,

Kansas so I could meet her parents. The car had holes in the floor-board. We got a little splash every time we hit puddles from the rain.

When we got to her parents' house, there was a tornado warning and bad storms in the area. We all had to go to the basement right away. What a way to get to know your future in-laws!

On the way back to Lincoln, her car broke down. We were supposed to go to a Dan Fogelberg concert that evening. We humped it to a farm and called a friend in Lincoln. He came halfway to the Missouri border to rescue us. We still made the concert!

Unlike me, Paula took school very seriously and studied most nights the rest of the semester. After graduating, she took a job in Kansas City. It didn't take long for me to experience feelings I had never felt before. I couldn't explain them, and they got stronger the less we saw of each other.

I moved back home from Lincoln to Columbus for the summer, and worked long hard hours for a construction company. I thought about Paula all day when I was working. We talked on the phone at least weekly and wrote letters often.

One day, I decided I wanted her to be mine. I was going to buy my first ring for a girl. It was going to be my promise or engagement ring. I guess I really didn't know the difference. I knew it when I saw it. A black-stoned tiger's eye. It was definitely unique, just like Paula. I liked being different too. Not to mention it was all I could afford. It cost about $150. I knew I wanted to marry her, and I knew she was the one that God had for me. There is still no doubt in my mind about that!

After about a year of living in Kansas City, Paula interviewed for a job in Omaha, so we could live together while I finished school and she started her career. While she was at her interview, I sat at a bar for a few hours, near downtown Omaha, with a friend of my dad's.

Her interview went well, and she was offered a job. We decided to drive to Columbus and celebrate! Things were coming together!

Once in Columbus, we went to a bar where my dad hung out. We had a few more beers. I remember playing pool with the County Attorney, as I continued to drink.

Still not ready to call it a night, we decided to go to a nightclub where there was dancing and more people our age. As I told my dad we were leaving, he said, "Let Paula drive, you are in no shape to drive." I wish I would have listened that night. We were not far from the club when I saw red lights flashing behind us. I was driving Paula's new car (not the lime green Chevette!). Not good!

Apparently we had a headlight out. I'm sure the Missouri license plates didn't help either. The police officer had me step out of the vehicle. I knew I was toast! I failed the field sobriety tests with flying colors! I couldn't say my ABC's, and seconds later had cuffs on.

After a couple of disagreements at the police station, I took an official breathalyzer and blew a .247 BAC. Again, not good! Man, what was I thinking? I wanted to go into law enforcement and now I had a DWI. Why don't young people think?

They let me out without bail since I was well known in Columbus. When I told my dad the next day, he was ticked! "I told you to let Paula drive", he said. I was thinking I would rather get the DWI than let Paula get one, although she had not been drinking the hours I had while she was at her interview.

To make a long story short, I lost my license for six months and got six month's probation. A couple of years later, I went back to court with a great attorney and got my DWI annulled. For a hefty price, I got it completely expunged from my record. They don't do that anymore.

After living together in Omaha for a short time, Paula began to be convicted by the Holy Spirit. She started missing going to church. One day, a married couple from my high school, Mike and Sheryl, helped us move some furniture. They had recently met Jesus Christ, and they spoke to us individually about it, while driving down the road. Girls were in the front of the truck, and guys in the back!

They had been raised in the Catholic Church, as I was, but they were bringing up debate points which I could not answer. Things like, "why do I confess my sins to a man, such as a priest?", and "why was I baptized as a baby, before I could even understand what baptism was?", and several other Catholic practices that were not included in the Bible anywhere.

Mike and Sheryl started holding Bible studies at their house, and invited us. I had fallen away from my relationship with God while in college. I had never heard the things they were talking about, but I was also fine with where I was with the Lord.

Paula was a little more interested. She started meeting with Phil and Tammy, another couple from the Bible study, and began really studying the Bible. I had no problem with her doing that, but I didn't feel the need to join her.

One night Paula came home from her Bible Study and told me she had gotten "saved". My first thoughts were to protect her from this couple who could be trying to brainwash her into some type of cult! She went on to explain she gave her heart to Christ. She was excited, and I was confused! I was glad that she found something new and exciting for herself, but I wasn't really open to listening to her, or talking much about it.

Then she dropped a bomb! She said we couldn't live together anymore. "What are you talking about?", was my first reaction. She went on to explain we were living in sin and had to stop. Oh my, these people had really messed her up! At the same time, I felt my mother nudging me. I knew if she was still alive, I probably wouldn't be living with any female.

Even though I didn't know how this would work since we were both broke and could hardly pay rent while living together, I tried hard to understand what Paula had been told by these church people. I had been in church all of my life. I was required to go to church every day before school. I was an altar boy. But I never heard of these things she talked about... having eternal life, being saved, and salvation, being unequally yoked.

To temporarily accommodate Paula's demand to live separately, I moved out of our apartment, and into Phil's basement. I started reading the Bible a lot. One night I was trying to disprove some of the stuff Paula was telling me. As I read in the book of 1 Peter, verse 2:24, it hit me like a ton of bricks:

"He himself bore our sins in his body on the cross, so that we might die to sins and live for righteousness; by his wounds you have been healed." 1Peter 2:24

Now, the Holy Spirit was working on me. I clearly understood what salvation meant. I got on my knees and cried out to God. I asked Jesus into my heart. Tears ran down my face as I felt his grace and mercy upon me, and a burden lifted. I knew in my heart and professed with my mouth that "Jesus is my Lord"! I felt as light as a feather! I was His and He was mine, and no one could take that away.

I wanted to tell Paula right away, but suddenly I was overcome with hunger. I left Phil's place, stopped at Taco Bell to satisfy my craving, and headed for Paula's. Immediately after telling her all about it, we started making wedding plans. We were married a few months later.

I always wanted to have a relationship with someone that I could totally open up to. No secrets! To me, that was true love. I struggled so much with this. That's why it was so special to me when I met Jesus personally. There were no more secrets! He knew EVERYTHING about me, and still loved me in a way that no one else could.

CHAPTER 6

Joltin Johnny

DURING MY LAST year of competition as an amateur boxer, I really began liking the pro game. It was exciting. I started traveling to some pro shows with Ray, a pro-boxing trainer and manager. He coached Ray McDermott, Johnny Bell, and a few others. They boxed all over the United States.

Ray's guys were spunky, crowd-pleasing boxers that didn't necessarily win all of the time, but always showed a lot of heart. They went out and fought their tails off. They were warriors! They traveled into the opponent's territory and gave the up-and-coming hometown heroes an opportunity to show off for their fans. It wasn't always showing off though. Ray's guys could cause an upset at any time!

Sometimes Ray's guys fought pro under alias names, for different reasons. One did it because he was still boxing at the amateur level. No one is allowed to participate in a sport at the amateur and pro level at the same time. The pro fights were more fun since there was no pressure, and a guy could make easy money doing something he loved. But when he actually won, he messed up someone else's record, and got a win for someone who didn't exist.

There were times when Ray's boxers didn't like boxing under the alias names. They felt like frauds. Once, in Indiana, one of them fought a guy who was a United States senator. The senator was well known for his amateur accomplishments, and was now fighting pro. He got all kinds of press. He had a huge hometown crowd rooting for him.

The senator must have been 15 years older than Ray's boxer but was really in shape. He hit slow, but solid. Ray's guy hit him a bunch, but only hurt him once the entire four rounds. "The Senator" won.

In the van, on the way home from the fight, the Paul Harvey Show was on the radio. Paul Harvey talked about the senator's fight for the first five minutes of his show, the whole time referring to the alias name from Lincoln, Nebraska. I couldn't tell anyone it was me!

Another time, it was necessary to really dig for excuses to cover actual identities. It was a show that was covered by ESPN and fight announcer Al Bernstein. Before the bouts Al was doing interviews with the boxers so he could show small clips during the fights. We told Bernstein one of Ray's fighters was wanted on a bunch of misdemeanor warrants and couldn't do the interview. ESPN couldn't show this particular undercard fight. We promised Al he was turning himself in when he got back home.

The pro post-fight parties were great. The boxers were treated like celebrities, signing autographs and visiting with fight fans and groupies. Once we stayed in Denver for three days after the fights. We spent everything we made fighting, but, man, was it fun! I really developed a liking for the Mexican community there. The guy putting on the boxing shows allegedly had some ties to the Mafia. If he wasn't Mafia, he was the closest to it that I would ever meet!

One of my favorite trips was to Wichita, Kansas. Coach Ray, Sanchez, and I were there. Ray McDermott was fighting. The local guy was undefeated and built like a pit bull. But, what seemed like an easy win for the hometown guy, turned into a classic Rocky fight!

Both opponents found themselves on the canvas several times. Between the third and fourth rounds of a four-rounder, McDermott's corner was telling him to "just get out, your getting hit too much". But he wasn't ready to go down. I really don't know how he kept going, but he had a lot of pride and thought he could beat this guy.

As the bell rang to enter the ring for the final round, McDermott struggled to his feet and Sanchez cheered him on, saying, "You got him this round!". The toe-to-toe slugfest continued for the entire three minutes. McDermott was faster, but the pit bull hit a lot harder.

McDermott had pretty good ring sense and knew when there was about a minute left in the round. He gave every ounce of energy he had, in every punch. He later shared that he was motivated by visions of his all-time favorite boxer, Roberto Duran, dancing in his head.

With just seconds left, McDermott caught the pit bull with a right hand/left hook combination that dropped him. McDermott knew he hit him very solid because he could feel the burn in his elbow. The pit bull went down hard. McDermott was exhausted and could barely stand. As he leaned on the ropes, he heard the count of 8..9...10! He turned around to see the pit bull still crumpled on the canvas. It was over! I won by knockout!

The decision hadn't even been announced when the hometown fans began firing hot dogs at me. I had to be protected on the way to the dressing room. Wow, what a brawl. The crowd loved it, and I loved it!

Another boxing trip, Johnny Bell was relaxing next to a hotel pool, just trying to get his head right before the fight. A couple of pretty girls came to the poolside and made some small talk. Johnny couldn't believe they thought he was "all that'. They sat next to him in their bikinis telling him how cool it was that he was a fighter and in town for a boxing show. They made him feel like a hero. They were really laying it on thick. They told him he was too handsome to be a fighter, blah, blah, blah. They said they had never been to a fight and wanted to know if Johnny could get them tickets. Sure, why not? Johnny didn't mind bringing a couple of his own groupies to the fights. What an ego builder!

At the fight, the girls were dressed to kill, and gave all their attention to Johnny, as did everyone else in the place! After the fights, Johnny took his groupies out to dinner and then went back to the hotel. Sitting in the hotel lounge, they finally laid it on Johnny. They wanted to show him the time of his life! Johnny couldn't believe this. "Ba.. ba..both of you?", he thought. "Am I really all that?" Yes! According to these pretty girls, he was all that! And it would only cost him $500! Oh, was Johnny Bell a naive guy! These girls were pros. He got strung along all day, thinking he really had it going on! Johnny, shocked, kindly let them know he was not interested. Since they weren't very good at taking no for an answer, I pulled the "I've got to go to the bathroom" disappearing act, and never saw them again.

Another time in Denver, after Johnny Bell fought, we were just hanging out, enjoying the fight atmosphere. Some girl walked up to Johnny and said, "Hey! I watched you fight in the Midwest Golden Gloves a couple weeks ago in Omaha!" Johnny told her she must be mixed up. Here he was, fighting pro under an alias, and he couldn't let anyone know he was still fighting amateur also. She said "No! I saw the boxing gloves tattoo on your right shoulder!" Sh#%! How do you explain that? She was right! His gig was up. The next day, I made the announcement before I got kicked out of the boxing game completely. I was turning pro, under my own name.

A couple of my pro fights were against the same opponent, a guy rated 6th in the United States. He gave me a lesson both times, but the cash made it worthwhile. He was a tall lanky Mexican who was a great boxer, and a real gentleman. A lot of pro boxers never get the chance to fight a guy of this caliber in their whole career.

The first fight, he stopped me in the 3rd round. The second fight was right after I met Paula. He knocked out my front tooth (also in round 3)! The punch wasn't enough to make me fall, but I got scared, choking on my tooth, so I took a knee. Try spitting a tooth out past a mouthpiece when you are choking! I remember taking the knee so slowly that he hit me going down. Wow, thanks! I really needed that!

Coach Ray wanted to stop the fight when I staggered back to the corner, but I wasn't stopping until I had given it everything. I had nothing to lose at this point (except maybe another tooth!). I hoped I could land that one lucky punch to turn the fight around and make a name for myself. At the very least, I was going over three rounds this time.

He stopped me again. In the 5th round this time. The doctor checked me. I told him I was okay. He allowed me to continue, but my opponent could smell the victory, and finished me before the round was over.

After the fight, my first thoughts were of Paula. What would she think? I made my way to the pay phone before I even showered. It was difficult to get a private moment because of all the groupies and press. I remember having to cover my face to hide the emotion when she told me she would still love me "with a front tooth or not". There was no doubt in my mind that she loved me for who I was, and I wanted to marry her. I think this was the first time I really considered marriage. All the way home, I thought about us being married.

Even though I didn't have a great pro boxing career, I had a lot of fun experiences. I met a lot of celebrities, and boxed on undercards with most of them. Harold Brazier, Donny Lalonde, Virgil Hill, Vampire Johnson, Jeff Franklin....I was once gloved by ex-light heavyweight world champion Marvin Johnson. I fought on a card with Tracy Patterson and was able to spend some time with his dad, Floyd, who was my dad's favorite boxer from the old days. One of my best memories had to be with Randall "Tex" Cobb. We fought in Lincoln one night and then drove all the way to Indiana to fight the next night. What a blast! He was probably the neatest boxer (and now movie star) that I've ever met.

After being married for a few years and starting a family, I decided it was time to let go of some things in my life and be a family man. Not only did I get out of the Army National Guard after eight years of service as a sergeant in the Military Police Unit, but I made the decision to retire from boxing. Several of my boxing buddies were getting slow and punchy. I didn't want my kids to have a punch-drunk guy for a father.

To make it official, I had a retirement party at a small West Omaha tavern. A lot of my friends came to share memories, a big cake, and lots of alcohol! It was a special night, but I drank too much. I remember Paula getting mad at me after we got home because I was taking a leak in the bathroom and was peeing in the trash can instead of the toilet. I must have really had to go that night because I wet the bed too!!

Retirement from boxing was not easy. It's hard to separate yourself from something that has been such a significant part of your identity for so many years. I actually came out of retirement twice. The real, final, last fight was seven or eight years after Paula and I were married. We were on a rocky road and were separated. I was broke and desperate, so I went to North Dakota to fight for some quick money. I wasn't in any fighting shape. I just did some tough rounds with a kid that needed the record.

My face was a mess after the fight. My eyes and nose were swollen. I made the mistake of trying to blow my nose, which, instead of making me feel better, blew up my face like a balloon.

I have no idea why, but I was driving the van home from North Dakota to Lincoln, Nebraska after the fights. It was a cold winter weekend. I was driving fast because I just wanted to get home. And there they were…the flashing lights behind me. The cop walked up to the van and shined his light in my face. He did a double take and said, "What the hell happened to you?" I tried to explain, as the other fighters in the van snored away. He let me go with a warning, and thankfully didn't check anybody for identification. One of the other fighters had warrants, and another was on parole and was not supposed to leave the state. I was now a correctional officer and was not supposed to be associating with felons, parolees, their families, etc. Things could've gone downhill very quickly. Anyway, I made it back home with hundreds of dollars for rent, and never put on gloves for competition again.

Over the years, even when I was fighting pro, I followed the Golden Gloves tournaments. In '96, I got the itch! Glenwood, Iowa, where we were living at the time, was known for a great wrestling program so, why not start a boxing club?

I started the club in my small garage, but before long, I had a place on the town square above a doctor's office. It was just a large room that had a bathroom, but I didn't have to pay rent or utilities. A couple of friends built a ring, and we were set. Soon I had some kids training, including my son and daughter. I worked at the prison all day, then went to the gym to train fighters for two hours every night.

It was a Christian boxing club, where we talked about Jesus to the kids, and tried to get them into church. Our team prayed together before any of our fighters got in the ring. We also held them to a high standard when it came to their behavior and attitudes.

The Club traveled to shows on the weekends as we could afford it. I spent a lot of our personal money for food and hotels, but it was worth it. Our team made a name for itself. Other coaches knew my fighters were in shape and ready to go!

In general, the Glenwood Boxing Club did very well. It was great for the town, and we had some great talent. I didn't put anyone in the ring unless they were ready. As a coach, I wasn't as tough on the kids as my coaches were on me. I wanted them to have more fun than I did. They would just quit if it got too hard anyway.

I coached Jay to the National Silver Glove tournament. He lost in the finals. I also had three kids win Novice Golden Glove titles. I had a super heavyweight who was a Glenwood troublemaker. Pete changed his ways when boxing got in his blood. He trained hard and was tough. At 6' 2", 250 pounds he didn't have anything but muscle and a hard head. He won two Novice Golden Glove titles himself.

It probably comes as no surprise that my favorite fighters were my own kids! I admit I was a little biased. My son had his first fight at eight years old and 47 pounds. It's really hard to coach and corner your own kid. I hated to see anyone land a good punch on him. As soon as he gave up other sports, and concentrated on only boxing, he really began to develop into a great fighter. He was a counter puncher. At some point he turned a corner and lived, ate, and breathed boxing. In 2007, he won the National Junior Olympic title. He represented the US Junior team at the World Cup tournament in Baku, Azerbaijan. He came back ranked 10th in the world. A short time later he was signed by a fight promoter out of Chicago. He got to fight on four World Title undercards on HBO. He finished with a 10-2 (8 KOs) record. He was a much better boxer than I ever was.

My daughter also grew up in the gym. She taught herself how to box by watching others in the mirror. As a result, she was a southpaw. She eventually started competing and won the Ringside World Title in 2005. This was the first time I cried happy tears as a father and trainer.

One evening, several years after the Glenwood club was up and running, the phone rang. It was Kenny Wingo. Kenny had run the notorious Downtown Omaha Boxing Club for decades. I first met him when I was boxing in high school. Our team made the trip to Omaha to spar his guys in preparation for tournaments. He was also instrumental in starting my boxing club in Glenwood.

Kenny told me he had some real health issues and he wasn't going to be around forever. He had problems getting up the steps to the gym. He asked me if I would be interested in coming and coaching for him. He wanted me to learn his program and take over his gym when he was gone.

Wow, I was speechless. I highly respected Kenny. For me, that was like getting a call from Tom Osborne to coach for the Huskers! "What am I supposed to do with my club? I asked. "Close it.", he said in his rough, grouchy voice. "If those kids want to box bad enough they will come to Omaha".

Paula was staring at me, and she could see on my face that something exciting was happening. I told Kenny I would have to think and pray about it and hung up. What? What?! It took me a while to get it out. We both ended up crying tears of joy! I'll never forget that moment!

I closed my gym, and donated all my equipment, ring, mirrors and other odds and ends to Servando Perales, who had started a Christian gym in Omaha. He had just moved from his garage to a building and needed more equipment.

I immediately started coaching at the Downtown Club and learning Kenny's program. Every gym runs differently. Every kid has different things that motivate them, hinders them and guides them. I wanted to fit in and show them all the love Kenny had, but I had big shoes to fill. I had recently started a new job in Omaha, so I went from the hospital, where I was the Security Manager, straight to the gym, every day. It took a few weeks to feel comfortable, but I got along with everyone pretty well.

One of the reasons I was excited about Kenny's gym was the financial security. Kenny had some financial backers. Most of it was from pickle accounts. I spent so much of our personal money to support the Glenwood club, so I was hoping things would get better in that area.

I had been with Kenny for about seven months, had gone on plenty of trips with him and the team, and was comfortable, when Kenny told me he was sick and needed to have a "little surgery:" A couple of days later, he said the surgery was scheduled later that week. He said if he didn't make it, that I shouldn't change much, but could implement my Christian stuff. I had hung a couple Christian motivation posters in the gym since I started and tried to talk to Kenny about Jesus once in a while, but he never said much about it.

I stayed at the hospital in the waiting room when Kenny went in for surgery. What started out to be a two-hour procedure had now turned into four, then six hours. I finally demanded an explanation! A doctor explained that Kenny had a tear that couldn't be repaired and wouldn't stop bleeding because of the blood thinners he was on. An hour later, he passed.

When I got the news, I was in the waiting room with several of the veteran boxers from his gym. I literally had to pry some of the kids off of Kenny when they said their goodbyes that night. They loved him so much. He practically raised a couple of them. My kids had a great love for him also. My daughter still announces his birthday, and the day he died, every year.

I left the hospital that night and didn't know what to do? Not long ago he had asked me to coach, and now, I was the new Head Coach at the famous Downtown Boxing Club. I just became responsible for the oldest and busiest gym in Omaha. I drove away from the hospital and soon found myself parked outside the Club. I sobbed and prayed for a long time.

Soon after Kenny passed, the two guys who were the supposed silent partners, the financial backers, started showing up at the Downtown Club. One of them had helped Kenny coach from time to time, and he started coming up and coaching while I was there. He began telling me how things were going to run. I explained to him that Kenny told me how things were going to run, and I would handle it. He said something like "Well, Kenny isn't here anymore!"

I knew things were not going as Kenny planned. He told me that these behind-the-scenes guys were on board with me running the gym. It was obvious they were not. I shared my situation with Servando, the founder of Victory Boxing Club. He had actually boxed for Kenny for many years. Soon I decided I had to leave the Downtown Club to eliminate any hate or hard feelings with this guy who was making things miserable for me and wanted to take over the gym.

And then, another call came. Servando wanted me to be his head coach at Victory Boxing Club. What perfect timing God has! I happily left the gym where I wasn't wanted, and for the next 10 years I trained boxers at Victory Boxing Club.

Victory Boxing Club was a Christian club, like the Glenwood Club. We ran a tight ship and held kids accountable for their actions at boxing and in life. We had Bible studies, were active in the community, and had a bunch of fighters. I made a lot of friends at Victory and loved the environment.

After using a dumpy gym without real heat or water for a few years, we got a great new building we converted into one of the best gyms in the Midwest. It was big enough to host shows, and we held plenty.

God's thumbprint has always been all over the Victory Boxing Club. After several generous donations, the building was paid off. It was in South Omaha and most of our fighters were Mexicans who could fight. On Thursday nights, we shut the gym down a half hour early and those who wanted to could stay for Bible Study. It was the only church some of them got. We saw lots of kids give their hearts to Christ.

Not everything was always great at Victory. We lost a kid to suicide, lost some to prison, and one to a drug overdose. Overall, we saw many more positives though. We had some join the service. A couple, including my son, became police officers, and others got college degrees.

During my time at Victory, I got very involved with some administrative aspects of the Nebraska Boxing Association. I eventually was named Vice President, and later, President of Nebraska Boxing. It seemed the more involved I got, the less I liked amateur boxing. I had to make some tough decisions as President, and there was no way to keep everyone happy. I started to see how the strong personalities of boxing coaches made the sport decline. The cliques and the backstabbing were unbearable. It was a relief when my term as President ended. I slowly became less involved, and after 10 years as head coach, I left the Victory Boxing Club.

Well, you can call me Ray McDermott, or you can call me Johnny Bell, or you can call me Joltin Johnny Determan! I have a few other alias names I used as well. There were so many that I lost track of them! But, one thing for sure, boxing is in my blood.

CHAPTER **7**

A Dream Come True

AS A KID, I dreamed about becoming a police officer. I was about 13 when I joined the Columbus Junior Police program. I stayed involved until I aged out. I rode with officers five or six hours at a time, going to all kinds of calls. There was nothing better than the rush of driving down the road as fast as you want, with lights and sirens going, and everyone moving out of the way.

One night I was out riding with a sergeant. We followed a van that was all over the road. Sergeant flipped on the red lights. The van kept going for several blocks, but eventually pulled into a driveway. Sergeant jumped out and approached the van. The driver hopped out also. I recognized him as the dad of a kid I knew. Sgt. tried to talk to him, but he just staggered toward his house. As Sgt caught up to him and put a hand on the driver's shoulder, he turned around and pushed the Sgt. I couldn't believe my eyes! Before I knew it, they were on the ground. The driver was big, and he was on top, punching Sgt. I got on the radio and started screaming, "An officer needs help!" The dispatcher tried to calm me down and said, "Johnny, tell me where you are?" I told him the street name and said we were right by St Bon's Church. I was so excited and scared that I gave the right street, but the wrong church. The dispatcher asked again what church we were near. Finally, I was able to process and tell him the

70

right name. The whole time we were having this conversation, Sgt. and the driver were wrestling. Finally, Sgt. got a hand free and hit the driver on the head with his five-cell flashlight, knocking him out. He was then able to handcuff him. Backup arrived shortly thereafter. The driver went to jail.

May 1987, after six long years of on-again, off-again college, I was finally graduating from the University of Nebraska with my Criminal Justice degree. My dream of becoming a police officer was getting closer. Tom, a buddy in my National Guard unit, was working in a prison. He shared a lot of good work stories during our weekend drills. Since the prison was hiring, I thought maybe I could use it as a stepping stone to get into law enforcement. I got hired, spent four weeks in the academy, and then officially became a State of Nebraska correctional officer.

My first week was unreal, especially in the chow hall, where all of the inmates gathered in one place. What was I doing here?! I was a "new fish" or "new jack" or "screw" to the inmates. But there I stood, just a kid fresh out of college, monitoring men of all sizes who had been convicted of serious crimes! I had no weapon, very little back-up, and no experience. I was uneasy to say the least, as they glared and checked me out from head to toe.

But, after settling in, I became an aggressive officer. I learned the rules and regulations backwards and forward. My philosophy was to enforce the rules in a firm, fair, and consistent manner. Some staff supported my methods, but others not so much.

It didn't take long for me to realize that I had some instincts other staff just didn't have. I found more drugs, sent more inmates to segregation, and was responsible for more loss of inmate's good time than most other staff. After just four months, I was promoted to Corporal, and after my first year of service was awarded the title of "Rookie of the Year". I had developed a reputation. Both staff and inmates knew what I was about…mostly!

Barely into my second year, I was patrolling the perimeter on night shift. A rabbit kept setting off an alarm at the north gate. Each time it sounded I had to check it out. About the tenth time, I was done. I got out of my patrol truck and grabbed a large rock. The Central Control officer was watching me on camera. I threw the rock up and over the top of two fences. It dropped and hit the rabbit directly on top of the head! The rabbit started going into convulsions. It dragged itself toward the fence. Central Control got on the voice box and lost it. He couldn't believe it, and neither could I. The rabbit finally got close enough to the fence that I was able to grab it, bleeding profusely. I drug it out from under the fence and threw it in the back of my truck. On my next round I threw it in the woods. End of story, I thought.

About 0800 hours the next morning, the phone woke me from a dead sleep. A lieutenant informed me that the morning maintenance worker found a trail of blood from the north gate. At first the higher-ups thought there was an escape, but somehow they came to the conclusion that I brought in a pellet gun to kill the rabbit.

The investigation went on for about three days. They were not buying my version of the story. I admit it was hard to believe. I didn't want to get my witness involved if he didn't have to be, but I had no choice when they decided to bring me up on charges. He was the control room officer that night, and a trustworthy veteran employee. As soon as they interviewed him, I was cleared of any wrongdoing. Only Officer Determan!

During those early years, drug interdiction was weak at the prison. One evening I was supervising visitations, and I spotted a visitor pass a bag of weed to an inmate. It took some convincing, but the lieutenant finally listened to me. We escorted the inmate to the lieutenant's office and strip-searched him. He stood there buck naked, holding his underwear in his hand, saying, "See, I ain't got nothin'." My heart sank, and the lieutenant's face was indescribable. Suddenly, a light bulb went off! I told the inmate to shake out and drop his underwear. When he did, I could see the bag wrapped in his hand!! He was good. He hid the stuff in the waistband of his underwear, then hid it in his hand during the entire search. It was a quarter ounce of weed. We called the cops while escorting the visitor to the front. Our policy was that we could not hold anyone for any reason, not even for the police. Can you believe that? A visitor committed a felony in our prison, and we couldn't hold her. So, we delayed walking her to the free side until the cops got there.

Neither my supervisors nor the cops knew what they were doing. It was like it was the first time it had happened! They didn't even know it was a felony to introduce marijuana into a state prison, yet it was posted on the sally port doors!!!

The visitor received a citation and was released. She eventually went to court and was sentenced to nine month's probation. The inmate went to segregation, pending investigation.

This was just the first of many drug interdictions I was involved in. Each incident, we learned a lot, and improved our processes. Eventually we were successful through the prosecution stage on both civilians and inmates.

The next issue to tackle was dirty staff. Some of the prison workers had no business being there. It was obvious which ones just wanted a paycheck. They worried me because I couldn't count on them to back me up in a tough situation. One lady was oblivious to everything around her. The inmates called her mom or ma or grandma. She acted like their mom!

We had no search procedures for staff. They could make a ton of money If an inmate talked them into bringing in weed or other drugs. For example, when tobacco was outlawed, a staff member could make $100 easy for bringing in a pack of smokes. Over the years, random searches and UA's on staff became procedure. Another way that contraband entering the facility was reduced!

After a couple of years as corporal, I was promoted to Caseworker. Instead of working on the yard, I was in a housing unit. The housing unit I was assigned to was officially called J1, but nicknamed Jungle 1. You can imagine where that name came from! I decided I was going to clean it up. My partner was a guy who didn't really want much inmate conflict, so he took care of the day-to-day duties while I did most of the security. We worked well together and had a lot of fun. I did a lot of shakedowns, found a lot of contraband (including drugs), and wrote a lot of misconduct reports.

One of our inmates was constant trouble. He was the only inmate I knew who had a 2-20 year sentence for burglary. He added more than five years to his original sentence because of bad behavior. He hated white officers. He wrote grievances on staff for anything. One day shortly before rounds, I had just been cussed out by him, and was outside the unit, near the back doors. I looked down and saw a small garter snake. My mind raced a little, and I picked it up and stuffed it in my pocket. I started rounds, and the stars were aligned that day. His cell door was open, and he was nowhere around. My load got a little lighter, as I casually walked past his door. When I had to take count about a half hour later, he was on his bed screaming!

As I continued working in the housing unit, a young guy, who was very good at what he did, became my boss. He ran a tight ship and didn't cower to the inmates yet knew what battles to fight. To me, everything was still black and white, by the book, like they taught in the Academy. I was aggressive, and the inmates filed a lot of grievances on me. My boss had to investigate those grievances, and counsel me occasionally. But, even though I was always in the middle of controversy, I was doing a good job and they couldn't argue that. They just never had an employee like me before. Through those counseling sessions, he taught me discretion. His wisdom impacted me and my career significantly.

One grievance that sticks out in my mind is when about 300 inmates signed a petition claiming that I was racist, among other things. They sent it to the Governor of Nebraska. An internal investigation was ordered. One day a big shot out of Lincoln showed up at the prison to interview me and the inmates. He was a total jerk to me. It seemed like a case of "guilty until proven innocent". He questioned me about allegations of targeting inmates based on race. I believed I just concentrated on the troublemakers and dopers. Many of them happened to be black. From my point of view, I didn't see color, just inmates and staff. He asked if I shook down more black inmate cells than whites, and if I requested more drug tests on blacks than whites? I had no idea. "I just try to do my job to the best of my ability", was my response. He assured me that he was going to dig up all the records on cell shakedowns and drug tests. I left the interview thinking I could be doomed!

Several weeks later, I was exonerated of any wrongdoing, including any racial profiling. The records did not show that I shook down cells or did drug tests disproportionately. However, the State felt they had to take some sort of action to pacify the powers that be. So, on paper, they required me to go to sensitivity training. I agreed to it, even though I felt I did nothing wrong. They never scheduled it, and I never went.

Not long after that whole ordeal, I got into an argument with an inmate, and called him a snitch. Of course, he wrote a grievance. I received written counseling and was told using the word "snitch" anywhere in a prison was unacceptable. Less than three weeks later, I overheard the Warden talking with a few people. They were laughing and joking. There was an inmate trustee, or porter, as we called them, in the area when the Warden shared a story and used the word "snitch". I froze up! I stood there staring at him! He didn't know what was wrong with me. That day I learned that the rules don't apply to everyone.

After a couple of years in the housing unit, I made Sergeant. I took on the Disciplinary Sergeant role. The Disciplinary Sergeant supervised the inmate property, disciplinary court, and the armory. My favorite part was running the internal court system. The inmates didn't care for me in this position either. I knew what it took to make a good case against them, and I made sure we had our ducks in a row before court. Since I knew the rules and laws better than most staff, I often advised the disciplinary chair members, on the charges, and appropriate consequences. The sanctions ranged anywhere from a verbal reprimand to loss of good time. The inmates had a right to legal representation at their hearings, and a right to cross examine witnesses. But, even with that, unless an officer wrote a very weak ticket, we almost always got a conviction.

I was also in charge of all the evidence and drug testing program. I was certified by the State Patrol to test controlled substances. The inmates hated me, and hated that I could test the substance, and then submit a report against them. Many of them tried to appeal this procedure, to no avail.

After about five years of running things inside from an office, I got hungry to go back to the yard. I took a Custody Sergeant position. I hadn't been in the thick of things as a sergeant before. Now I was supervising the yard, and officers. I waited until I got off of probation in the position, and then I went to town.

Shoes were the easiest way to pay off a guy for dope or store items. You just order the shoes in the size of the guy you owe and give them to him. He either doesn't put an inmate number on them or puts his own number on the shoes. Either way, it's illegal. I directed yard officers to set up outside the kitchen, and check inmate's shoes for numbers. Sometimes we got 10 pairs of shoes in a night. Controlling property in prison is huge. Most staff don't realize it.

I really took pride in this position. I always made sure my uniform looked good and I had a shine on my boots. Rotating shift every six months was rough, especially the overnight shift. But we made the best of it. Lieutenants didn't work weekends, so sergeants got to run shift. My buddy Tom and I lifted weights in the middle of our area checks. Once, while the inmates were locked in their cells during a bad winter storm, he bet me five dollars I wouldn't run barefoot in the snow from one end of the yard to the other. Of course I did it!

We had a lot of fun, but never jeopardized the security of the institution. One of our responsibilities was training staff on emergencies and procedures. Teresa was new and working Central Control. One night after all inmates were locked down, we decided to test her. We set off a body alarm, a fence alarm, and a fire alarm, all at the same time. We really freaked her out! But she handled it well. She went on to become a captain later in her career.

One night, Tom and I made plans to go out after shift (0600 hours!) for eggs and beer. We drank all morning. A blizzard was moving in, so we decided to head home. I told Tom he had to come to the grocery store with me first. I had to get diapers and several other things before going home. Paula and I lived in the country at the time, and we needed to be prepared if we got snowed in.

Tom and I went to the store, still in uniform, with quite a buzz on. We goofed around and got all the groceries, and then headed to his apartment in my 4-wheel drive truck. I wouldn't drive him up a hill to his apartment because it was too slick and steep. I told him to get out. When he refused, I put my truck in park, got out, opened his door, and pulled him out by his coat. It was really icy. We were falling all over the place.

When he finally realized I really wasn't going to drive up the hill any farther, he grabbed several bags of groceries from the bed of the truck and threw them all over the parking lot. It sounds immature and stupid, but we thought it was pretty funny. Now the joke was on me, sliding around the parking lot trying to pick up groceries. He got the last laugh!

After several years as Sergeant, I spent a few years as Lieutenant, and then took a newly developed Emergency Preparedness position. I was part of a group that taught Emergency Preparedness to the entire Corrections department across Nebraska. We also developed and implemented emergency exercises.

Once, we were doing a hostage exercise that had been going on for over eight hours. As one of the developers of the exercise, I chose to be a hostage taker. I had prior experience with our Hostage Negotiation Team, so I had the advantage of knowing a lot of their procedures.

The hostages and I were in a large stone, high-rise building surrounded by our department SORT (Special Operations Response Team). A negotiator talked me into releasing hostages periodically throughout the day. All hostages but one had been released. It was almost dusk, and I had an idea.

As a diversion, I instructed the last hostage to run out of the front door. I slithered out of a ground level crawl space, and inched on my belly into the weeds that surrounded the building. I was able to get into some lower ground about 100 ft from the building and pull tumble weeds on top of me. I couldn't believe I made it out! Totally undetected!

I heard the SORT guys get ready to do a tactical assault on the building. Soon I heard flash-bangs, and knew they were clearing each room and floor. I laid as still as I could. I heard the team asking where I could be. They were irritated when they realized I had escaped, and they needed to search the grounds.

They formed search lines and started moving through the weeds. As I laid flat and motionless on my back, one of the SORT members approached. My heart was beating so loud I thought I could hear it. His eyes got huge as he almost stepped on me. Before he could move, I raised up and grabbed the end of his rifle, trying to wrestle if from him. In less than 15 seconds I felt a heavy boot hit my ribs. Several SORT members were on me before I could take another breath. They restrained my arms and legs in flex cuffs. After a few more cheap shots, they brought me to my feet and escorted me away. I could see the anger in their eyes. I had made their team look bad. The exercise was announced completed and terminated.

I went to California for a three-week training class with several emergency preparedness specialists from other prisons around the state. When we finally got some free time, we decided to tour Alcatraz. It was a spectacular sight that could only be reached by boat. We weren't there very long when my curiosity was stirred by an area marked "Restricted". I decided I needed some pictures and crossed a small barrier. Looking around, I locked eyes with a guard. He quickly approached and escorted me directly back to the boat. At the boat, we were joined by a second guard who sat next to me across the water to landside. I was asked to show an ID and was permanently banned from Alcatraz. I'm thinking there must be a statute of limitations and I should try to go back there someday.

As an emergency specialist, I worked on drug interdiction when I wasn't training staff. Visitors tried to smuggle drugs into inmates during visits, and sometimes tried throwing them over our perimeter fence. Besides the Missouri River levee behind the prison, there was also a paved road that led to a nightclub and a couple of huge ships on display, called Freedom Park. Inmates arranged for their contacts to drive down the road, and throw contraband into the prison yard.

We developed intelligence from inmate phone calls and letters, if we could decipher their codes. We hid our vehicles, and positioned ourselves in bushes and weeds on the back side of the levee, about 300 yards from the nightclub. Then we waited. As a suspicious car approached the back of levee, we busted out of the brush and detained them.

One summer night, Sgt Doug and I were on the lookout. The nightclub was closed, so there wasn't much traffic. That seemed to be when we had most of our action. Although we were not officially allowed to carry a gun, I always had mine with me when I was on surveilliance assignements. I wasn't about to die trying to stop dope from entering the prison.

A vehicle came down the paved road. It approached so fast we were almost spotted. Doug and I quickly ran for cover in different directions. The vehicle backed in less than 20 yards from us, against the trees and tall weeds. Doug ended up laying down on a piece of aluminum that was under the weeds, so he couldn't move without making noise. I landed several yards in front of him.

The door opened on the car and out stepped a very large man. He went to the back of his vehicle and lit up a cigarette. I tried to get as flat as I could in the weeds because he was now only about 10 yards away from me. He walked around, smoking his cigarette, then moved toward the front of the car. As he moved, I moved, sliding on my stomach backwards to get better cover. Still on my belly, I reached down to my waist to check for my gun. It was gone!

The guy loitered around, and lit up another cigarette. My heart was racing. I was no longer armed, and I didn't know what this guy would do if he spotted us. As he sat on the hood of his car, I belly crawled back up to where I thought I lost my gun. I found it.

The guy started to move again. This time he walked to the driver's door and got in. He sat for a few minutes, then started his car and left.

What a rush! Doug and I got up out of our hiding places, with a great sigh of relief. We laughed about our close call for a long time. We had many more adventures behind the levee, and made several interdictions resulting in arrests.

Late in my career at the prison, I had a freak accident at home. I was standing in my yard, with my dog, when a stray came into our yard. My dog took off chasing the stray. They made a big loop around my yard, then came running back toward me. As fate would have it, the stray, a sturdy black lab, wasn't watching where he was going because he was worried about my german shepherd on his tail, and he ran right into my legs, sending me airborne. My right leg was broken.

I yelled for Paula in the house, but she couldn't hear me. I crawled, in total agony, across my front yard to the door. I laid on the ground, pounding on the door, when she found me. Several hours later, we left the hospital with my leg in a full cast.

I took a couple of weeks sick time and stayed home eating pain pills and playing playstation. I tried to figure out how I could go back to work with a full cast on my leg. Suddenly, I had a brilliant idea! If I could learn to drive with my left leg, and get to work, I may be able to convince my boss that I could still do surveilliance on the back side of the levee.

After a bit of convincing, the major allowed me to work as close to eight hours a day as I could handle, sitting in my vehicle, collecting intelligence. I had a 2-way radio and could communicate with the tower and perimeter patrol vehicle if I observed anything suspicious.

The first day was rough. I couldn't stretch my broken leg and get comfortable for very long. However, the owner of the neighboring nightclub came through for me. He didn't hesitate to let me use a limo he had parked inside a locked fence. He knew we were doing drug and contraband interdiction back there.

He gave me the combination to the gate, and a spare key to the limo. I didn't need to drive it, but needed heat occassionally since it was late October in Nebraska. This was much more comfortable than sitting in my personal vehicle.

For the next two weeks, I went to work, parked my car near the nightclub, hobbled on my crutches to the gate, unlocked it, and crawled into the limo. I basically just chilled all day. Sometimes I stayed the entire shift. I had binoculars, and was able to collect license plate numbers of possible suspects. I caught a nap or two, and even worked on this book, kicked back in the limo.

Climbing the career ladder at the prison, I never forgot about my dream to be a street cop. I tested for a few different police departments and kept waiting to get a call. I was still working in the housing units when I got a call from the Omaha Police Department.

I had tested a few months earlier and did very well. Out of 1200 applicants, I was 43rd on the list. They were going to hire 60. "I made it!". I got lightheaded. My lifetime dream was about to come true.

But wait... the guy on the phone wasn't finished. Due to affirmative action, I had dropped to 66th. I couldn't believe it! My heart sank. I had heard a lot about affirmative action but had never been directly affected by it. There was a quota to fill. It didn't matter if I scored better on the tests and the interview. They needed females or other minorities, and I was screwed. This devastating news definitely called for a stop on the way home and several beers! Eventually, I convinced myself that I was happy where I was. I rationalized that I really didn't want to leave our acreage and move within the city limits anyway. Life went on.

About three months later, I got another call from the Omaha Police department. It was the same guy who called before. He told me that several of the minorities were unable to pass a special reading and writing test, and I had moved back into the top 60. He offered me the job. This time, Paula was pregnant and due in three weeks. I didn't feel I could leave her to go to the Academy, which was scheduled to start in a month. I turned him down on the spot. I would stay at the prison.

A prison is really a city within a city. What began in 1984 as a 240-bed minimum security prison was now a medium security facility that had doubled in size. I dealt with drugs, gangs, sex, fights, theft, and assaults...the same crimes dealt with on the streets. The positions I held at the prison allowed me to act not only as Officer, but also as Investigator, Gang Specialist, Sergeant, Trainer, Armory Supervisor, Lieutenant, and Emergency Preparedness Specialist. I really didn't miss out on my dream at all. My dream, and so much more, came true!

CHAPTER 8

To Protect and Serve

WHILE I WAS content working at the prison, I have to admit, my curiosity was stirred when I found out the county in Iowa we had just moved to had a deputy reserve program. I applied and was accepted to the Mills County Sheriff Reserves. After a bunch of classes and a year of OJT, I was ready to go.

A minimum of 8 hours/month was required for the reserve program, but I usually worked 10 or 12-hour shifts, so that wasn't a problem. On a good night, there were four deputies working. Most nights there were only three, and often the third would be a part-timer like me. Sometimes on Friday afternoon, I went straight home from the prison, and was in a patrol car on the road by 5:00 p.m. I looked forward to working special events like July 4th, or RAGBRAI. I would put in 30 hours over the weekend easy.

Mills County included 437 square miles that ran along I-29 in Iowa. The Reserve Department grew to about 12 deputies. Eventually, I held the offices of Vice President and President. We also took on a contract with the County DNR (Department of Natural Resources) and helped police the parks and hunting areas. We got paid for the hours we worked for them.

My FTO, Mike, was one of the best deputies on the department. He was also the K-9 officer. He wasn't one to mess with if you were a bad guy. Once, we stopped a guy and saw dope in his ashtray. Since he wouldn't get out of his vehicle, my FTO pulled him out through the car window.

I was nervous riding with him the first time. He was rough on me. I wasn't familiar with a lot of the county roads yet. In the middle of a conversation, he would stop suddenly, and say, "Tell me where we are! We're getting shot at! We need help! Where the hell are we?" I failed miserably on most of those scenarios. I got many lectures about how important it was to always know my location.

One evening we drove down a road to a little lake, looking for dopers. Finding it empty, we drove slowly down the lane to leave. He asked me how I was with my firearm. I had already qualified, and done pretty well, so I confidently replied, "I can hit what I'm shooting at."

Not a minute later, he stopped the car and said, "There's a rabbit on your side, about two o'clock. Shoot it!" I thought he had to be kidding. He wants me to discharge my weapon at a rabbit. As I sat there a bit confused, he again said, "Hurry up! Shoot it!" I didn't know if he was setting me up, if it was a test to see if I would obey him, or if he really wanted to know how well I could shoot!

I drew my weapon, took aim out of my window at the rabbit in the thickets. He again yelled, "Shoot that thing!".

I shot....and missed. My heart sank.

He put the car in gear and started down the road, ranting about how he wasn't sure if he wanted me backing him up if I couldn't hit a stationary rabbit. I felt horrible and said nothing. Next thing I know he was aiming out his window at a rabbit. K-bam! He fired off a round and the rabbit tumbled. Not only did he hit it, but he also blew its head off! As he holstered his weapon, he said, "That's how you need to shoot!" He was rough, but he trained me up well. We became very good friends.

This was the beginning of 12 years of working as a deputy as often as I wanted. It was in the late 90's when meth was out of control in the Midwest. I did a lot of drug interdiction and ended up being in a lot of the action. I was involved in some good pursuits, a shooting, a couple of suicides, numerous drug search warrants, lots of investigations, traffic enforcement and an undercover sting that made the news.

The shooting incident I was involved in was at an apartment building. A kid was shot in the head. I was just leaving the Sheriff's Department when the call came out. I wasn't sure I heard it right since there was rarely a shooting in this area.

I was one of the first to arrive and was advised by dispatch that the shooter had left the scene. I ran up the steps to the apartment, hearing screaming and people yelling frantically. The door was open. As I stepped in, I recognized the kid laying on the floor in a pool of blood. The scene was chaotic. Several people were talking at the same time, all trying to tell me who the shooter was, and what he was driving.

Another officer arrived and directed me to escort the victim's ambulance across town to the football field where the life flight helicopter was going to land. The victim was then airlifted to a hospital.

All officers were on the lookout for the shooter's vehicle. It wasn't long before another deputy radioed that he found the car abandoned at a campground by the Missouri River. I raced there, lights and sirens!

The Sheriff and some state troopers arrived to help in the search. With guns drawn, we cleared the suspect's car and then formed a line to walk the woods along the river. One of the troopers had a dog that was trained in tracking. After about 15 minutes, the dog picked up a scent and led us to the riverbank. He took us right to the edge. He was going crazy.

The shooter was hiding in some underbrush. With about 10 guns pointing at him, he was ordered to climb up the bank. I holstered my gun and cuffed him, while the Sheriff continued giving commands. The shooter was arrested and later convicted. The victim lived but was never the same because of brain damage. The gun was never recovered because it was thrown in the river. All because of drugs!

I kept myself busy doing road patrol and traffic enforcement when not taking calls. The training I had from the prison in drug recognition proved to be quite helpful. I arrested a lot of drunk drivers. In fact, so many that I received an award from MADD (Mothers Against Drunk Drivers) two years in a row. It wasn't uncommon for the full-timers to make traffic stops and request that I come and perform impairment or drug recognition. Most of my arrests were very solid. I was seldom beat in court.

One year, on New Year's Eve, a man was driving on the shoulder and wouldn't pull over. I pulled up next to him, with lights and sirens, and pointed him over. When he finally pulled over, I walked up to his car and could tell he was totally smashed. I finally got him to crawl out of his vehicle for a breath test. It was cold and snowy. When he blew into the portable breath test machine, he passed out and fell backwards into a snow-covered ditch. It wasn't easy, but I eventually got him to jail. He was a riot during the interview process!

Another night, at dusk, I drove up a one-way, lonely, beer-drinking road. A car was parked at the end of the road. I ran the plate before getting out of my cruiser. The owner of the car came back 10-99, "wanted", out of another county.

I got out of my car. No one was visible in the other car. I drew my 9mm Smith and Wesson, and slowly approached it. Through the window I could see an open, long barrel gun case and some shot gun shells on the seat. The hood of the car was still warm. He hadn't been here long. My heart pounded as I thought about being in his sights. I scanned the heavily wooded area and worked my way back to my car. I radioed my findings and asked for backup.

Sometimes it could take 15 minutes for another deputy to arrive. I was scared and started to pray. "Oh God, please don't let tonight be my last night on earth". My wife and kids filled my mind.

I decided not to sit and wait. I thought I might be harder to hit if I was a moving target. I picked the right side of the wooded road and walked in, about 25 yards. I moved slowly, quietly, and tactically. Some of the video games I played with my son raced through my mind!! A silhouette of a person started to come into view. I raised my weapon and yelled at him. He appeared to be crouched down. I couldn't really tell if he was looking at me through the trees. I kept my weapon on him as I circled to his flank. I took cover behind a large cotton tree, continuously yelling commands.

I could now see he was holding a gun. Again, my heart raced! I tried to take slow breaths. If I was going to shoot, I couldn't miss. He had a long gun and could hit me from this range.

He would not respond to any commands. His head wasn't moving. I could see his profile. I continued to move forward from his flank. Now within 10 yards, it appeared he had passed out and the gun was resting on his arms. My thoughts ran wild. What if he was a decoy and there were more guys with guns?

I could hear sirens in the country air, but help was still miles away. I looked around for something to throw at this guy. I wanted some kind of reaction out of him. I found an empty Mountain Dew bottle. I picked it up and made the best throw of my life! It hit him on the shoulder and then bounced off his head. He immediately tipped over on his side, and that was it!. No more moving! Continuing to get closer and yelling commands, I could see blood. He had shot himself.

I couldn't reach dispatch from my portable radio, but soon my back-up arrived. I don't even remember who it was, but I was freaked out, and glad to have a partner there. I helped tape off the crime scene before the Sergeant sent me back to town to get the coroner. A couple of troopers were now arriving.

I picked up the coroner at his office and rushed to get back to the scene. I had lights on, and passed a few cars, when the coroner said, "What's the hurry? He's already dead!" Lol! I was so pumped I wasn't thinking straight.

When I returned to the scene, the investigators had discovered a design the victim made in the dirt. It was a circle with a line midway through. They speculated his plan was to pull the trigger when the sun hit the line. As I'm checking out the dirt, one of the investigators said, "Well, he must have had one last Mountain Dew before he popped himself", pointing at the bottle I had thrown at him! I didn't say a word, but definitely squirmed, thinking about my fingerprints on that bottle. Apparently, the bottle was never printed.

Another night, when I was actually at home, and off-duty from both jobs, I heard a call on the scanner of a shooting at a house I could see from my front door. I grabbed my gun and badge and sprinted to the house, as the first cruiser arrived. We were met outside the front door by a fellow reserve deputy. He was calm, and said, "My wife just killed herself. She's in the den."

We walked in the house to see a young female, in her 20's, sitting in a chair with a gunshot to the head, brain matter splattered nearby. I couldn't believe my eyes! A large handgun, that appeared to be a 357 Magnum, rested across her lap with one of her hands still on it. We left the room and sealed it off until DCI could get there to do the investigation.

In the living room, the husband was calmly smoking a cigarette. Things just didn't seem right here. I looked around the house a little bit, and then, as investigators arrived, I left to write my report.

A couple of days after the incident, a search warrant was done on the house. Plastic surgical gloves were found in a trash can. Of course, the husband had some ridiculous story explaining the gloves, and he couldn't be disproved. I still believe, as do the parents of the girl, that this guy murdered his wife. The case was closed as a suicide.

Another time, in our same little neighborhood, in the middle of the night, there was a "shots fired" call. A kid had an AK-47 type rifle and was shooting multiple rounds.

A city officer and a deputy were the first to respond to the address. As they approached, the kid opened fire on them. The deputy's car was hit several times when he reversed away from the rapid-firing rifle. The car looked like something out of a movie with torn metal and shattered glass. The deputy, who would later become the Sheriff, was hit in the hand, losing a finger.

The city officer was advancing on foot, when the shooter's dad tackled him. He was taken into custody before he could do any more damage.

The next morning, I helped protect the crime scene and look for shell casings. I don't remember exactly how many were found, but there was a bunch. I'll never forget the feeling I had when I saw how shot up the Deputy's car was. It was a wake-up call...how quickly things can go wrong in this line of work!

One warm summer night, right about dusk, another deputy and myself responded to an assault in progress several miles across the county. I followed him, lights and sirens. We traveled east, the sun at our back. I was about 50 yards behind. We were approaching 80 mph. Out of nowhere came a car from the south county road. I couldn't believe my eyes! They ran the stop sign and were instantly t-boned by my partner.

Everything went slow motion. I slammed on my brakes, mouth wide open, not believing what I was seeing! Upon impact, the metal twisted, the tires squealed, and both cars spun into the ditch. Somehow, I safely parked and turned off my siren, as I called on the radio for fire and rescue. I told dispatch we might as well get life flight on the way too! I knew we would need them!

I sprinted to the ditch, both cars steaming and making noises I couldn't identify. The front half of the deputy's Crown Vic was demolished. My partner moaned and groaned, but at least that told me he was alive. I couldn't see him clearly. He was trapped.

The other car, a smaller compact car, hissed and smelled of gas and anti-freeze. I felt like I entered a sick movie when I looked through the missing driver's side window. There was very little blood. The driver was almost fully on the lap of the passenger. It was a couple of teenagers. I ran to the passenger side. I started checking pulses, but I was shaking so bad I couldn't tell if it was my pulse or theirs! Another deputy arrived and checked the pulse of both. They were clearly dead.

I stood by my cruiser for a minute, trying to review things in my mind.

I was in shock. I wished I had something to drink. My mouth and lips were so dry that I couldn't swallow. Rescue units were arriving. They started to work on prying my partner out of his car. The sirens kept coming. We had to shut down the highway. Finally, he was in the ambulance, getting help.

A short time later, as I stood at the side of the road, a car came to a sliding stop in the gravel right behind my cruiser. It had pulled around the long line of stopped traffic. Two young girls jumped out of the back seat and ran toward me. Before a word came out of their mouths, they started hitting me. I was still trying to clear my head and wasn't quite sure what was going on. They started yelling things that I couldn't process, as they continued to beat on me. Then one clear sentence made its way through their tears. "You killed our brother!"

It was a long ugly night. The state police did a total reconstruction of the accident, even moving the cars back to the point of impact. I have a photo of the re-created scene. The conclusion was that the deputy was going 81 mph, and the teens died on impact.

I was interviewed by the crash investigation team, but don't remember a thing I said. My head didn't clear for weeks. Nightmares continued for months. My partner was permanently disabled and never able to work as a deputy again.

I have seen plenty of death, but telling others about the death of their loved one is a whole different ball game. One of the worst cases I was involved in was the mom of a young kid killed in a car accident. Our department was notified of the death from out-of-town and was asked to notify the parents.

A full-time deputy, Evan, and I, got the call. We met at the address. We were both familiar with these situations and neither of us wanted to do it. I can't remember if we played rock, paper, scissors, or if it was because I was a reserve and he was a full-timer, but I was the one who got the dreaded honors.

We walked up to the trailer and knocked. A woman opened the door, staring at us as if she knew what was coming. I cleared my throat and began to tell her that her son had been killed. Time stood still. She looked right through me. Then she collapsed. I caught her and held her up. There was not much I could say. I told her I was sorry, and my prayers would be with her.

We just stood there as she continued to sob. She asked for details, but we didn't have any. I didn't make a traffic stop the rest of the night. I was sick for her loss and prayed for her comfort.

It wasn't uncommon for my K-9 deputy buddy, Mike, to call me when he got paged out on a search warrant. I lived just around the corner from him, so he picked me up at all hours of the night. I got great experience on drug investigations.

During the 90's there was a huge meth problem in our area. The first time I went along to serve a warrant, we found a bunch of jars with some liquid in them. I removed a cap and took a sniff. I thought I was going to die! It burned my lungs so bad! I think it jacked me up. It was precursor that was ready to go in a batch of meth.

We also found several 10-gallon buckets of urine while searching the house. During the interview of one of the house members, I asked what the buckets of urine were all about? She told me everyone peed in the same bucket at their tweaking parties. Then, to make the next batch of meth 10 times stronger, they used a turkey baster to take urine from the bottom of the bucket where all the excreted meth had settled.

I rarely worked weekend mornings, but the one time I did, the body of a missing person was found in the river. The Sheriff and I worked it together. We pulled her out of the water. Thank goodness it was a little chilly out and she was just starting to get a bit stiff. Limbs can literally fall off a drowned person that has been hot and weathered and in the water for a long time. We took her to the morgue, and watched the coroner start his examination. The cause of her drowning was unknown.

Some of my best memories working as a deputy were during the summer, at a problem lake along the interstate. It had low water levels and people could drive to nearly any place around it. Lots of partying and drug use went on, sometimes all night long.

There was a two-week stretch when Evan and I parked our cruisers and walked in. We walked up on a lot of things on that little lake! One time, two people were under a blanket, not moving. As we approached, it was obvious they were making out. We loudly announced "Sheriff's Department". The blanket flew off and two heads popped up. Much to our surprise it was two females!

Most nights we made drug arrests, just walking from tent to tent, or bonfire to bonfire. One night we had three felony drug arrests in a row. After getting one booked in, we returned for more! If we walked up on a campsite with a bunch of minors drinking, we usually ended up in a foot chase. Actually, we were entertained as they ran through the woods in the dark. We didn't try very hard to catch them. We were after the drug users.

Probably the most constructive thing I did for the Sheriff's Department and the Mills County people was an undercover sting on homosexuality or "park perverts" in a roadside park.

There was a place right off the highway that had walking trails and a couple restrooms. One holiday afternoon, President's Day I think, my son and I were playing catch in the parking lot while my wife and daughter walked the trails. My son needed to use the restroom. When he walked in, he interrupted two guys messing with each other. He got my attention and called me over. I ran, and met one quickly leaving the restroom. I barged in to find another pulling up his pants while standing in the middle of the small wooden structure. I yelled at him, and ran him out.

We played ball for another hour or so and saw several other men meeting in the bathroom. It was obvious to me what was going on. The next day I went to the Sheriff and told him what I had observed. I asked if we could do an undercover sting. He said he didn't think he would have any volunteers. I said I would do it, as long as I had back-up. He gave me the go ahead. I was pumped. I was going to do some uncomfortable police work and run these guys out of our county!

The first time I went to the park, I really didn't know what I was going to do or how I was going to do it. I parked my personal car near the restroom and sat for a while and thought about it. My backup said he was in place on a gravel road about a quarter mile away. I made sure I had my gun concealed well, and a portable radio in the car.

As I sat there, a car rolled in, and a guy got out. He walked to the restroom. Before entering, he stopped and turned directly toward me, nodded his head, and gave me a wink! Wow! "Here we go", I thought. "I think he wants me to join him."

Since I didn't research any case law before starting the sting, and the Sheriff didn't offer any pointers, I was going into this kind of cold. I turned on my mini tape recorder and put it in my front pant pocket. I walked into the bathroom toward the urinal. The guy was behind the next partition. I acted like I was going to urinate. Then he walked around the partition with his pants down and his penis out. He asked me to hold it. Wow! I couldn't believe it! Instead of holding it, I identified myself as a deputy, and pulled out handcuffs. I told him to pull up his pants and face the wall. OK! So, I had my first one! Wow, how easy was that?! I called my backup in and loaded the guy up! We charged him with indecent exposure.

Looking at the laws, It seemed indecent exposure and criminal trespassing were the two most appropriate charges. I got him booked in. He had a pretty hefty cash bond to get out. Turned out he was a married with a family from a nearby town and was a family crisis counselor!

I returned to the roadside park. Within an hour I had my second pervert. He was a nurse from another nearby town. As soon as I got my badge out and identified myself, he went for the door. I grabbed his arm and did a straight arm bar takedown on the hard concrete floor. I walked him out cuffed and stuffed before I even had time to call my backup.

While walking out, another guy was walking in. When he saw us, he did an about face and almost sprinted to his car. I was high with excitement, having my second in custody. I yelled, to the guy scurrying away. "Ya all come back now, you hear?"

That night at home, I checked my recordings. Both of them were bad. They were muffled. Not good! It's going to be my word against their's in court.

I contacted a deputy who worked for a task force in our area and asked him to work the sting with me. He agreed and got me hooked up with a good recording device that he could listen to live. I had the microphone/recorder on me in the restroom, and he had the listening and taping equipment in his car, but there was no way for him to transmit back to me.

The next time we decided to work the park, I felt much more prepared. Deputy Bo and I went over everything together. If someone exposed me, the code words were supposed to be, "That's a big one". That would be his signal to come rolling in from across the road and help me take the perverts into custody.

It wasn't long before a guy pulled in. I decided to go into the bathroom first. I stood reading the gross stuff on the bathroom wall when he walked in. He went to the urinal, took his pants down, and very obviously started playing with himself. I continued to read. When I turned slightly, I could see he was facing me. I turned all the way around, looked at him and asked, "What are you doing?". He just grinned... so I said "That's a big one". This apparently got him all worked up, and he began really going at it. His pants fell to his ankles. I displayed my badge and placed him under arrest. I patted him down and found condoms and lotion. As we walked out of the bathroom, my partner arrived. We got him booked in, and much to our surprise, he was another family counselor from Omaha. Unbelievable!

We set up again a couple days later. Bo had another task force member with him. We tested our equipment, and off I went. The code words remained the same. This time it was a Saturday morning. As I pulled into the park in my personal vehicle, I could see there was already a Cadillac parked near the restroom. I quickly got out and approached the building. As I walked in, I told my backups I was going in.

I walked in to find two guys standing there. They were both extremely big guys. There was one at the urinal who looked to be about 265 pounds and stocky. The other was about 6'3" and skinny. He was reading the walls. They both appeared to be in their 40's.

I said, "What's up?", and walked past them to the other urinal. I acted like I was urinating and then stepped back as I zipped my pants.

When I turned around, both of them were exposing. The tall one was blocking the door. The other one just turned around from the urinal and had his pants down to his thighs. He took a step toward me in this small room, as he masturbated.

Immediately I felt like I was in a really bad tactical position. I used my code words for backup, and told him "That's a big one", and he took another step toward me. As I backed up, he got closer to me, still playing with himself. I was quickly running out of space. Louder this time, I said, "That's a big one!".

Now, with my back against the wall, I once again said the code words! He was face-to-face with me and reached down and grabbed for my privates. I pushed him hard in the chest to get a little room and reached to my back for my gun. I drew down on him and quickly pointed at his partner who was still at the door pulling up his pants. I wondered where in the world my backup was!

I screamed that they were under arrest and had them lay prone on the floor to cuff them. I just started yelling, "BO GET IN HERE!" A minute or so later Bo and his partner finally arrived!!. "Where the heck were you?!". They were laughing so hard they couldn't talk.

I was really not happy with them, and I let them know. They just kept laughing as they explained how funny it was hearing me yell. "That's a big one!"

It turned out the two we arrested were homosexual roommates from yet another nearby town. They both worked as cooks at a country club…Yuk! I charged both of them with indecent exposure and criminal trespassing, and the one who grabbed me with an additional charge of sexual battery.

We also towed their cars when we arrested them. The main concern that had these two sniveling was some tropical fish they had just bought and left in the car.

We made a few more arrests and ended up with 10 arrests in 8 days. The sting had caught the attention of the media, both radio and newspapers. It started to slow down a bit so Deputy Bo and I decided to take our operation to another roadside park several miles away in a little farm town.

Shortly after we set up in our new position, a guy pulled up in a little pickup. I walked into the bathroom and soon he came in. I started reading the disgusting things on the wall and he started some small talk. He asked who the guy in the truck was and I said "Oh that's my roommate and he's really shy. He was like "The shy type huh? I like shy." He seemed turned on and started to expose right after that. He asked if my roommate and I would be interested in following him to his house? I grinned and agreed, thinking how I wanted to get revenge on my backup for showing up so late the last time.

We left the restroom. I got in Bo's vehicle and the perp got into his own. Bo blew a gasket when I told him we had a date at the guy's house. He tried to call dispatch to let them know we were changing locations as we started following the perp to his house. Apparently, we were too far out in the county to reach dispatch by portable radio. We were about 25 miles from where our dispatch center was located.

Bo was getting very uncomfortable as we followed the guy down a couple of county roads, and that made me happy. I told Bo the guy had a swing that he wanted to put us in. Bo was in a panic, and I laughed hysterically! I told Bo, "We're going to this guy's house because he likes shy guys, and I told him you were very, very shy. Once he gets you in his swing, we will arrest him."

Bo made the decision to take this guy down as soon as he got out of his vehicle in his driveway, since he had already exposed back in the park. I let Bo take the lead. It was my turn to sit back and laugh! "Go get him, shy guy", I said as we got out of our car.

We put him down at gunpoint right away. It was a good thing we did, because he had a loaded .38 on his seat. It was properly registered and not concealed, but I'm glad he didn't exit his vehicle with it. We never did get to swing!

The sting was all over the news. Eventually, word must have gotten out to the park pervert community, and the arrests died down. Before long, court hearings started, and they weren't fun!

Our county attorney was clueless. This was totally new stuff. I had gathered some information from some cop buddies in Omaha, and almost had to coach her. Since she let these guys' attorneys treat me like I was the criminal, I decided to take the Mel Gibson approach and defend myself. More than once I was threatened by the judge with contempt for my answers.

Once, a defense lawyer was keying in on the fact that I wore a pinky ring during the operation. Then he got on me for allegedly winking at one of the suspects (not!). Looking back, we should have used different code words. All of the defense teams keyed in on the fact I was saying, "That's a big one", and claimed I was enticing the perps with this language.

Some of the guys pleaded guilty to save embarrassment of a trial, and some of the cases got thrown out. A decision was made that the witness had to be "offended" in order for an indecent exposure conviction. But, a police officer can't be "offended" in his duties. Can you believe that? The most appropriate charge would have been lewd conduct, but, at the time, there was no such charge on the books. There is now!

I still have some of the court transcripts from the hearings. I can't believe the abuse I took on the stand. I also had to take a lot of vacation time from the prison and racked up 88 hours of court room time before it was over. Fortunately, I was getting paid for it.

It was the best of both worlds. I got bad guys locked up for a part-time gig, and I kept bad guys locked up full-time at the prison. But, there was a cost to fulfilling my dream. I have trust issues. I have been lied to, burned, and mistreated. I was backstabbed by co-workers, inmates, civilians, partners, kids, parents, and people from every walk of life. Who can you trust?

CHAPTER 9

More Crazy Memories

Hospital Security

AFTER YEARS OF service in Corrections and part-time Law Enforcement, I felt like I was ready for a change. Maybe it was time to slow down a bit. I started looking around. Late one night, I was surprised to see an ad for a Security Operations Manager for a local hospital system. The position reported to the Security Director, who happened to be a prior Nebraska prison assistant warden. I never worked with him, but I knew his name. Since I met or exceeded all of the qualifications, I decided to put in. I was still on crutches from my dog mishap, so I hobbled into the interview, negotiated for a little more money, and found myself hired.

The operation behind the scenes of a hospital was eye-opening. Thefts, domestics, shooting victims, and drug seekers, not to mention that we were the only hospital in town with behavioral services for both children and adults struggling with mental health issues. In my future, there would be many incidents with out-of-control patients and family members.

My position was new, so I got to develop my own agenda. I had a team of about 20 officers between three hospitals. Some were really good and some were slugs. At my interview, the hospital president suggested the security team's professionalism, or lack thereof, should be my top priority. Like a new football coach, I would take three to four years of writing and implementing new policies and procedures and increasing training. I enjoyed the challenge, and felt like I was making a difference every day.

One day, I was sitting in my office when the phone rang. "Hey, we just had a shooting reported in our front lot! I have no other information." I ran out of my office, straight to my car in the back employee parking lot. I knew I could get to the front lot quicker in my car than if I tried to run across the hospital grounds.

I drove up and down the rows, scanning the front lot, when I saw a lady standing and screaming. Next to her was another lady face down in a pool of blood. Since I didn't know where, or how many shooters there were, I approached carefully. The hospital didn't allow armed security, but I had my personal weapon next to me on the seat. It appeared there were no threats. I hopped out of my car, staying aware of my surroundings.

"Save her! Save her! Do something!"

I knelt down and turned the injured woman on her back. Her clothes were soaked with blood. It was hard to see where she had been shot. She faded in and out of consciousness as I radioed for fire and rescue and more security officers. All I could do is put pressure on her wounds until help arrived.

Fire & Rescue arrived in great time. They scooped up the patient, loaded her in the squad, and drove off. It took me a few minutes to realize why they were heading to a hospital other than ours, but we were not a trauma center, and that meant the lady was in critical condition.

As it turned out, the victim had been robbed. She was on her way into the hospital to visit her husband, who was dying of cancer. Someone asked her if she had a tire jack. She was kind and willing to help out. In return, the perp shot her, and stole her purse. All in a hospital parking lot! The lady lived; her husband died. The perp was never caught.

You never know what others are going through in a hospital. Less than 5% of visitors are at a hospital for something positive, like a birth. The other 95% are there for something bad. Instead of just wondering what a stranger's situation was when I got on an elevator, sometimes I offered to pray with them. Instead of passing by all the patient rooms, sometimes I stopped and prayed with them. A partner and I started a Bible study in the adolescent behavioral unit for a while. We had Bibles to hand out to any kid who wanted one. Unfortunately, the Bible study was terminated when my partner gave a Bible to a kid whose parents were atheists. They called the hospital to complain, and I was told to stop the Bible studies.

After 14 years of working for this great hospital system, Paula and I decided to move to Texas. My last week of work was a tough one. I was investigating a pharmacist for drug diversion. He was a young male in his late 20's. I didn't have anything solid except that his numbers didn't add up. His boss also had concerns.

I invited the pharmacist to my office for an interview and interrogation. The more we talked, the more deception I saw. Between his vague memory, his eye movement, and body mannerisms, I knew I had the right person. After an hour of denial, I told him I didn't believe him, but I believed he had an addiction problem that the hospital could help him with. I gave him my card and suspended him, pending investigation.

I escorted him out of the building and told him to call me if he wanted to come clean. I told him I might be able to save his job if we got him into drug counseling.

The next morning, I received a call from the police. It was a detective asking why they would have found my business card in this young pharmicist's pocket? He was dead. He had overdosed on a bunch of the pills he had stolen. The police found nine empty beer cans, some vodka, a list of nine different drugs adding up to 130 pills, and letters of apology. One of the letters was for me. It was a tough last case.

Scars

The first scar I got is on a knuckle. I climbed my neighbor's tree to look at baby birds in a turtle dove's nest. I was almost there when a branch broke. I fell, catching my hand on a sharp limb on the way down.

I was at a party at Issac Walton during high school. I was intoxicated and messing around with a guy. I was standing next to a building when he came at me. I backed up and was going to feint a punch at him. I didn't realize how close I was to the building. When I drew back, my elbow went through a window. I bled like a stuck pig and never went to the hospital. Someone put dressing and scotch tape on it, and we called it good.

I have a couple of scars above my eyes. Both from boxing. One was from a head butt while sparring. The other was a cut in the Golden Gloves where the doctor stitched me at ringside.

I have a scar between my eyes from an intoxicated episode in high school. My bedroom was in the basement at my house. It was a miracle I made it down the stairs to the light switch. I flipped on the light to envision a path to the bed across the carpeted floor. I flipped the light back off and headed for it. I knew I was getting close when I slipped, and went face down, hitting my head on the metal bed frame. I could feel blood, but I just crawled into bed and passed out. Several hours later I heard a scream and my name being called. I tried to open my eyes, but they were glued shut with dried blood. When I was able to force them open, I saw my mom standing over me with a look of horror on her face. I was covered in blood to my shoulders, and so were my sheets. I was cut bad and deep, but never got stitched.

My right cheek was scarred in a similar incident at my sister's wedding. After a few hours of partying on a boat, we butted up to a dock so the wedding party could continue on land. I stepped out and missed the dock with one foot. My face landed on a steel dock post. I ended up at the hospital and got a dozen or so stitches and had a cracked jaw. No wonder my dad always called me Two-can. It seems I have a problem handling alcohol.

Not all scars are physical. Some are mental, and no one knows how deep the cut really is. Many of my experiences have left mental images that haunt me. I pray, "God, please help my mind forget what my eyes have seen!"

Death

During my freshman year in College, I became close to a girl. We were getting a little serious, and I decided to throw her a surprise birthday party. I sat on the front porch, waiting for her to come home from her night class. As I watched her turn across the busy street in front of her house, she was t-boned. She died.

I was so blessed to be adopted by really great parents. I wouldn't change anything about where and with whom I grew up.

My mom always had a lot of medical problems. As a youngster I had no idea how bad some of it was. Early in life, she nearly died from encephalitis she contracted from a mosquito bite. While I was growing up, she always struggled with stomach ulcers. I was 20 when she died from a brain aneurysm. She was only 48.

Unlike my mom, my dad fought on until he was 83. After losing his second wife, he stayed busy golfing and meeting friends for a cold one afterwards. He also enjoyed his Husker football season tickets. I often thought he would die of a heart attack at a Husker football game.

Dad had prostrate cancer for a long time before he developed serious symptoms. Once he could no longer drive, my sisters did alot for him. My brother Joe spent alot of Sundays with him watching sports on TV, reading the paper, and eating good food.

Dad took part of my heart with him when he left us, but the wisdom he modeled in his strong work ethic, honesty, and integrity will be with me forever.

Regrets? Definitely! When I started college, Mom joked about me coming home just to get my laundry done. She teased about how I would come home, say hi, drop off my laundry, and be gone. She was right. I thought I had so many people to see.

Did I tell Mom I loved her enough? I know I didn't. When I left the house with my friends she always said, "Be careful, I love you." I never said it back because I didn't know what my buddies would think. Don't ever make that mistake!

Did I spend enough time with Dad? I don't think so. I would give anything to have another conversation about this week's sports stories.

One night we got a phone call that no parent ever wants to get. Our son Johnny was calling from the scene of a horrible car wreck that our daughter Jesi was in. She was unresponsive.

We had been in Hammond, Indiana that day, where Johnny had knocked out his opponent to make his professional boxing record 6-0. Johnny flew back to Texas, where he was living and training, and we drove back to Omaha. We were pretty worn out.

After that first hour of hard sleep, Paula's cell phone rang. It was the news I had envisioned and prayed against for so many years. I was screaming at Paula to tell me what happened! I could see her face and hear Johnny's voice. We dropped to our knees and prayed for God to help us, and save our baby girl!

We packed a bag as quickly as possible and checked airline flights. Nothing would leave until noon the next day. That wasn't soon enough for us. We had to get back on the road.

It was a long quiet trip, as we prayed silently and said little. The radio didn't work, and we only had one CD that we played over and over. Paula and I were lifeless, not knowing any details. When we finally got an update, we learned that Jesi missed a stop sign on the way home from a movie with three of her friends in the car. The truck was going 66 mph when it hit her. One of her friends may have been ejected. Jesi was being transferred to a trauma hospital in Dallas.

In the end, everyone involved survived, thank goodness! Jesi's brain was bruised and bleeding a little. She had actually weighed in for the Texas Golden Gloves tournament that morning. She was coming out of retirement, looking good, and bam! She was never able to box again.

I had been keeping my distance from everyone around me for many years. My wife, kids, dad, sisters, brother, and some friends. The thought of losing someone else close to me was terrifying. One summer, I laid awake, night after night, while Johnny rode motorcycles with his buddies. I can't eat or sleep when Paula travels without me.

Attachment disorder? Detachment? PTSD? I don't know what it's called. I just know it's a struggle, and I live in fear of losing someone else.

Football

As a youngster I played little league and freshman football. I'm not sure why, but I played dirty sometimes. In little league, if I was in on a tackle and at the bottom of the pile, I bit calves and ankles. As we got older and I was a freshman, I liked to pull leg hair to hear a guy scream. Of course, I acted totally innocent when they tried to accuse me. The key was to do it only when there was a pile. I was never caught and penalized.

Since I was a kid, I loved the Nebraska Cornhuskers. Attending many games and going to college there made me a diehard fan. I have good memories of games with my dad as a kid and good memories watching the game from the student section after partying for a few hours. I saw many great victories. Actually, I had one of my own.

It wasn't during a game and I'm not even sure it was football season. Bob, Tim, Goose and I were planning a roadtrip to Columbus. We had just left the courthouse in Lincoln where Goose had to meet with a judge over a past issue. As we cruised up N 10th Street in front of Memorial Stadium, we had to stop for a guy standing in the middle of the road. We honked. He didn't move. He just stood there giving us the finger.

"How dare him", I thought. I jumped out of the van and quickly approached him. He was clearly intoxicated and started talking smack. He called me some choice names and then started to raise his left arm. I was already in a modified t-stance, ready to fight. Rather than let him get his punch off, I threw a hard straight right hand to his jaw. He dropped like a bag of potatoes, going straight back, not even bending. He hit the concrete hard. His eyes rolled to the back of his head. I knew he wasn't getting up.

Fearing someone may have seen it all happen, I pulled him out of the roadway, jumped back into the van, and off we went. We pulled onto Cornhusker Highway and headed out of town. As we all laughed and joked about the great one-punch KO, part of me was scared I killed him.

We headed out of town on Cornhusker Highway. Suddenly, we heard a siren. We all four turned around at the same time to see the flashing lights behind us. It was a Nebraska State Trooper. We made our way into the slow lane to pull over. My life and future career flashed before my eyes. Apparently, someone had witnessed the brutal knockout and called us in.

As we pulled to the right and slowed down, the trooper came alongside our van, slowed down even with us, and shook his finger. He then continued down the highway at a high rate of speed. It took us a moment to realize he was just trying to get us to scoot over so he could go to his call!

When I got back to Lincoln a couple days later, I checked the newspapers to make sure there wasn't a homicide investigation going on. I came across a short article about an ambulance call in front of Memorial Stadium for an unconscious person. I assumed it was the guy who provoked his own destiny.

The Kansas City Chiefs were my favorite pro football team for a long time. They were the closest to Nebraska, and the games were usually a riot. Except for a couple...

My buddy Bob and I went to a game once, in some extreme heat. It was more than 90 degrees. I drank a little alcohol. At halftime, I decided to go on the concourse under the stadium to cool off. I got some water and a hot dog. After finishing both, I sat along a wall and apparently fell asleep.

Sometime later, I felt an unbearable strike against the bottom of my feet. I opened my eyes, and still in a fog, saw, and grabbed with both hands, what hit my feet. It was a nightstick that police used to carry. Grabbing the stick was interpreted as an aggressive move by the officer holding it. The next thing I knew, he maneuvered it under my arms and against my back. He managed to lift me up with it and walked me to the closest exit.

Once outside the door, he gave me a swift shove. Somehow in the maze of thousands of cars in the parking lot, I was able to find my pickup. I climbed underneath it to finish my nap. To the best of my memory, sometime later, Bob threw an ice cold drink on me. I woke up suddenly, and, trying to sit up, banged my head into the underside of my pickup frame. Down I went again!

One early fall Kansas City Chiefs game, I had a great idea for some fun during pre-game tailgating. There was a line of port-a-potties at the edge of the tailgating area. I brought bread ties specifically for temporarily locking people in them.

Some of the victims were good sports, and some not so good! Either way, it was fun to watch. They would panic and start banging on the door. When they finally pushed the door hard enough, the ties would break, and they would have freedom.

Right when I finally ran out of bread ties, I saw the best candidate of the day enter one of the port-a-potties. He was a big muscle-head, wearing a tank top two sizes too small. I frantically searched my vehicle, and found one of those miniature locks. I locked him in, and there was no getting out. The rest of the story isn't pleasant.

3-Wheelers

3-wheelers were never my thing. I drove two of them, and had a wreck on both The first time was at the annual Platte Center July 4th Demolition Derby. This annual event drew hundreds of people. There was a lot of partying all day long.

I had only been there a few hours but was plenty lit. A friend had his 3-wheeler there. The police didn't bother anyone riding around the fairgrounds, but leaving the fairgrounds on a 3-wheeler was trouble. I asked if I could take his 3-wheeler for a ride. And what a ride it was!

It didn't take long for me to get bored riding around the dusty fairgrounds. I couldn't get up enough speed! I was in the mood for some excitement. So, I got on a road leading out of town, twisted the throttle, and flew.

It was a hot summer day and the wind in my face felt great. As I came over a small hill my eyes locked in on a Platte County deputy sitting stationary, watching traffic. Even if he wasn't running radar, I knew I was toast. I had the 3-wheeler fully opened up and was moving.

To my left was a wide open freshly plowed field and to my right was a huge cornfield. I locked up the brakes and made a hard right into the cornfield. As I turned toward the field I saw the deputy's red lights heading my way.

In Nebraska, "knee high by 4th of July" meant a good corn crop. This was an exceptional year for corn! It was at least six feet high. I flew off the seat with every row, bouncing and trying to get deep in the middle of the field to hide. As I reached what I thought was a safe spot, I killed the engine. I sat for a few minutes to catch my breath, and to check out all of the cuts on my arms from the sharp cornstalks.

Not hearing any sirens or anyone stomping through the corn, I decided to get back to the fairgrounds. I estimated I had a straight shot through the cornfield back to crowds of people. I took off at a moderate speed, hopping over the rows and mowing down corn. Soon I could hear the roar of the cars from the derby. My plan was to get to the bleachers, jump off the 3-wheeler and mix in with the crowd.

As I reached the edge of the field, I could see the people and the bleachers. I gunned the 3-wheeler for my final approach. There was a clearing from the end of the field to the bleachers. I felt like I was home free with no deputy in sight.

By the time I saw the drainage ditch, it was too late! I slammed on the brakes, but went into the ditch full of water, nose first. The impact caused such a huge jolt that I couldn't hold on. I landed flat on my back. Things were cloudy for a few minutes. Several people ran up to see if I was okay. As my eyes came into focus, there was the deputy standing over me with a smirk on his face.

My friends helped me to my feet. I expected to feel handcuffs going on my wrists. Instead the deputy said. "I hope you learned your lesson", and seeing I was fine, he walked away.

I vowed never to get on a 3-wheeler again, until the next time! It was a few years later when I got on another 3-wheeler. Paula and I decided to spend the weekend on the river by my hometown of Columbus. The Platte River had easy access, great sandy beaches, and the water was low in the summertime. A buddy who lived close to the river let us use his 3- wheeler for the weekend.

We loaded up our tent, other camping supplies and some goodies, and off we went. The short trip was only down a road, over a levee, across some flood control rocks, down a small bank, and we were on the river. We found a toe head we liked that had shallow river channels on both sides, and lots of sand to ride around on.

After a couple of great days, it started to rain. We packed up and headed out with Paula on back, and all our gear strapped down. We made our way across the small waterway, over some rocks, and to the levee.

For some reason, going up the levee from the river side seemed much steeper. We were about halfway up when I felt the front wheel coming off the ground. In slow motion, we flipped backwards.

I did my best to hold the handlebars up, and make sure Paula didn't get crushed. She got out of the way, and the 3-wheeler came crashing down on my face. Specifically, my jaw.

We pushed the 3-wheeler over the levee and got back on it. I drove, in the rain, to the hospital. I was treated for a cracked jaw and some broken teeth.

On a lighter note...

In my late 40's, blows from boxing and shooting mortars in the National Guard, affected my hearing. The doctor said I had lost 50% of my hearing in one ear. I started wearing a hearing aid. Sometimes the hearing aid was annoying.

One night, I was getting comfortable, and decided to take my hearing aid out. I set it on the end table next to my recliner. A Nebraska football game came on later. I kicked my feet up and was enjoying a pile of peanut M&M's I had dumped on the table, totally engrossed in the game. My eyes never left the TV as I occasionally grabbed a few. But, I bit down on one that was very hard. It cracked into pieces, and I couldn't taste any chocolate. In just two bites, I had a $2000 hearing aid snack!

I have two birth certificates and two different names. I was born

Joseph Shuelke, and became John Determan when I was adopted. In my late 20's I decided to find out about my birth family. I was the product of an affair my mom had with the plumber. My sperm donor and birth mom had both already passed, but I found several half-siblings. I lived less than 20 miles from one of my sisters. Another was a meth and crack addict that lived in the county where I was a deputy, but I never arrested or had contact with her. And, yet another was an art teacher at my high school, but I didn't know her. Two other brothers: one was blind; I was able to meet the other brother. We had a lot in common, and maybe even looked a little similar. So, if I ever get in so much trouble that I need a new identity...

I voted for the first time when I was 55 years old. I thought one vote didn't make a difference, and I inevitably seemed to be busy on voting day.

I love pigeons. I had a couple when I was a kid, then again when my kids were growing up, and now, again, later in life. There is something about pigeons that warms my soul. They give me peace and tranquility. I love their personalities. The sounds they make, and the finesse with which they fly, give me joy.

I have several different colors of Homers. I can let them out to fly around and they will come back to their lofts. Actually, we can take them miles from home, and let them go, and they will make it home! I name them and get attached to them, but many have been killed by hawks or cats. Keeping them safe is always a priority.

Paula and I hope to start a small business during retirement with pure white birds that can be released at weddings. The name of the company will be "LoveBirds".

Once I took Paula and the kids on a family vacation to Mexico to visit some missionaries for a few days, and then spend a few days staying at a condo in Corpus Cristi, Texas. We were approaching the border when I started wondering if I had anything in the car that might be considered contraband. I intentionally left my gun at home, but, as my mind raced, I realized I always kept extra bullets in my console.

With one hand on the steering wheel, and the other digging around in the console, I tossed out all kinds of bullets, one by one, on the road to Mexico.

We finally got to the border, went through immigration, the search, and then tried to pay our fee to cross the border. Unfortunately, we forgot to notify our bank we were traveling, and our credit cards had been shut off. The bank was watching gas charges from Omaha, all the way south to the border, and suspected our cards had been stolen. There would be no entering Mexico on this day! We turned around and headed for Corpus Cristi a little early.

CHAPTER **10**

Conclusion

AS I END this book, a new chapter of life has begun. We now live in Texas, and Nebraska is no longer home. We are enjoying the life we have left with our children and grandchildren.

I am back into coaching boxing, since my son opened a gym. I still fish when I can, and enjoy my pigeons. I'm back working with bad guys, in a county jail this time.

I praise our awesome God, who let me survive all the craziness and near death experiences in my earlier life. I am convinced that God has kept me alive to spread His Word, and I give Him all the glory! I thank him often for giving me the perfect wife and two great kids, that have now grown to be adults.

I hope you enjoyed some of the "Secrets of a Simple Man".

Favorites

Food - Brisket

Color - Purple

Fish to catch - Northern Pike

Fish to eat - Walleye

Band - Aerosmith

Singer - Neil Young

Gun - Springfield XD

College Football team - Nebraska Cornhuskers

Pro Football Team - Minnesota Vikings

Birds - Pigeons and Pheasants

Sport - Boxing

Boxer - Roberto Duran

Therapy - Fishing

Soda - Mountain Dew

Soup - Posole

Animal to hunt - Deer

Day - Saturday

Candy - Strawberry twizzlers

Snack - Sunflower seeds

Lightning Source UK Ltd.
Milton Keynes UK
UKHW020632020821
388172UK00010B/784